KT-528-627

Layman's Bible Book Commentary
John

LAYMAN'S BIBLE BOOK COMMENTARY

LBBC

JOHN

VOLUME 18

James E. Carter

BROADMAN PRESS
Nashville, Tennessee

4211-88

ISBN: 0-8054-1188-7

Dewey Decimal Classification: 226.5

Subject Heading: BIBLE. N.T. JOHN

Library of Congress Catalog Card Number: 81-65391

Printed in the United States of America

Library of Congress Cataloging in Publication Data

Carter, James E., 1935-
John.

(Layman's Bible book commentary; v. 18)
1. Bible. N.T. John—Commentaries. I. Title.
II. Series.
BS2615.3.C37 1984 226'.507 81-65391
ISBN 0-8054-1188-7

DEDICATED
To the churches
that I have been privileged to serve as
pastor
Wise Memorial Baptist Church, Lena, Louisiana, 1955-57
John T. White Baptist Church, Fort Worth, Texas, 1958-61
Temple Baptist Church, Gainesville, Texas, 1961-64
First Baptist Church, Natchitoches, Louisiana, 1964-77
University Baptist Church, Fort Worth, Texas, 1978-

Foreword

The *Layman's Bible Book Commentary* in twenty-four volumes was planned as a practical exposition of the whole Bible for lay readers and students. It is based on the conviction that the Bible speaks to every generation of believers but needs occasional reinterpretation in the light of changing language and modern experience. Following the guidance of God's Spirit, the believer finds in it the authoritative word for faith and life.

To meet the needs of lay readers, the *Commentary* is written in a popular style, and each Bible book is clearly outlined to reveal its major emphases. Although the writers are competent scholars and reverent interpreters, they have avoided critical problems and the use of original languages except where they were essential for explaining the text. They recognize the variety of literary forms in the Bible, but they have not followed documentary trails or become preoccupied with literary concerns. Their primary purpose was to show what each Bible book meant for its time and what it says to our own generation.

The Revised Standard Version of the Bible is the basic text of the *Commentary,* but writers were free to use other translations to clarify an occasional passage or sharpen its effect. To provide as much interpretation as possible in such concise books, the Bible text was not printed along with the comment.

Of the twenty-four volumes of the *Commentary,* fourteen deal with Old Testament books and ten with those in the New Testament. The volumes range in pages from 140 to 168. Four major books in the Old Testament and five in the New are treated in one volume each. Others appear in various combinations. Although the allotted space varies, each Bible book is treated as a whole to reveal its basic message with some passages getting special attention. Whatever plan of Bible study the reader may follow, this *Commentary* will be a valuable companion.

Despite the best-seller reputation of the Bible, the average survey of Bible knowledge reveals a good deal of ignorance about it and its primary meaning. Many adult church members seem to think that its study is intended for children and preachers. But some of the newer translations have been making the Bible more readable for all ages. Bible study has branched out from Sunday into other days of the week, and into neighborhoods rather than just in churches. This *Commentary* wants to meet the growing need for insight into all that the Bible has to say about God and his world and about Christ and his fellowship.

BROADMAN PRESS

Contents

THE GOSPEL OF JOHN

THE GOSPEL OF JOHN

Introduction

The four Gospels are often represented symbolically by the figures of the four beasts found in Revelation 4:7. Commonly, the eagle is used to represent John. This is because of all the birds the eagle can fly higher and see farther. The eagle can look straight into the sun and not be dazzled. Of all the Old Testament writers the writer of the Gospel of John has the most penetrating gaze into eternal truths and mysteries. It is as though he looked straight into the eyes of God who sent his beloved Son Jesus Christ to the earth to redeem humankind.

Without doubt, the Gospel of John is the most loved and the most used of the Gospel accounts. There is a simplicity to it that speaks to the most humble Christian and a depth to it that challenges the most committed scholar. No one ever knows all there is to know about the Fourth Gospel.

The Gospel of John is also the most complex of the Gospels. Quite obviously it is written from a different perspective than the Synoptic Gospels (Matthew, Mark, and Luke are called the Synoptic Gospels because they take a similar viewpoint as though seeing together). In John's Gospel there is no account of the birth of Jesus, his baptism, the temptation experiences, or the ascension. Jesus' parables are not in John's account. But Jesus does speak in long discourses which are not found in the other Gospels. The order of events is even different sometimes, as in the cleansing of the Temple. John's Gospel puts this at the beginning of Jesus' ministry while the Synoptic Gospels place it at the end of his public ministry. Because of these complexities and differences in the Gospel of John from the Synoptic Gospels there are some questions that concern us. Who wrote the book? Who was the beloved disciple? What was its original intention? And this is what makes the Gospel of John intriguing, interesting, and imperative for an understanding of both the life of Christ and the Christian faith.

Appeal

Some have compared the Gospel of John to a pool in which a child can wade or an elephant can swim. It is both simple and sublime. It is both easy and complex. All believers are attracted to it and challenged by it.

Part of the appeal is in the special knowledge that the writer of the Gospel of John had that other writers either did not have or chose not to use. From John's Gospel the knowledge of such things as the turning of water into wine at the wedding feast in Cana of Galilee, the nocturnal visit of Nicodemus, the conversation with the woman at the well in Samaria, and the raising of Lazarus from the dead is gained. This Gospel is the one that gives insight into the character of disciples like Andrew who was always introducing people to Jesus and Thomas who often asked questions.

The appeal comes from the detailed knowledge that the writer had about the land of the Bible. He knew his way around Jerusalem. And he was familiar with the country through which Jesus traveled.

The touch of the eyewitness is in so much that the writer provided. The note of a particular time of day or the time sequence in which events occurred show up in this Gospel. And he gave such interesting touches as the observation that there were barley loaves in the little boy's lunch when five thousand men were fed, that there were six waterpots when Jesus turned the water into wine, and that the smell of the perfume filled the room when Jesus' feet were anointed at Bethany.

Actual chronology did not seem to interest the writer of John's Gospel as much as the significance of the events. There are places where the time sequence is left undetermined. As indicated already, he put the cleansing of the Temple at the beginning of Jesus' ministry while the other Gospels placed it at the last. The synoptic writers place Jesus' crucifixion on the Passover Day. John dated the crucifixion at such a time that it would have occurred at about the same time the lamb was slain for the Passover meal on the day before Passover. These things have caused some interpreters to question the historical accuracy of the Gospel of John and to rearrange many of the events. Others, however, have come to take more seriously

John's chronology. Chronology as well as the situations described and teachings recorded all fall into a purposeful pattern in this Gospel account.

Author

The Gospel of John is actually anonymous. But many attempts have been made to identify the author of this popular Gospel account.

The traditional understanding has been that John the Apostle, the son of Zebedee, was the author of the Gospel of John. Part of that reasoning goes back to the statement of Irenaeus, an early church father (about AD 200) who identified John as the apostle who leaned on Jesus' breast at the Last Supper. He indicated that John had written the Gospel. Added to this is the identification of John as the beloved disciple which many see (although not all interpreters think it was John) as the touch of the eyewitness. Also the author's use of "I" and "we" contribute to the thinking that John the Apostle was the author.

Others take the position that it was written by someone named John but probably not John the Apostle. Again, going back to the ancients, Papias was quoted by Eusebius in his *Ecclesiastical History* as having known of a John the Elder in Ephesus. He was also supposed to have known of the tombs of two people named John in Ephesus. Tradition is very strong that John the Apostle ended his days in Ephesus and that is where the Gospel of John was written. Taking this into consideration, the writer of the Gospel is identified with John the Elder in 1 John. It is thought by those who take this approach that while John the Apostle may have been behind the book, it was actually written later by John the Elder.

The third major view fails to find any individual as the author of the Gospel of John. These interpreters identify a circle or a school of people who were followers and students of John the Apostle. From this group, possibly with more than one writer or an editor, the book was compiled later after the death of John himself.

No one actually knows precisely who wrote the Gospel of John since the book itself does not identify the author. Creditable contemporary New Testament scholars hold each of the three approaches to authorship outlined above or variations of them. However, the actual human author is not nearly so important as the spiritual truths preserved in this Gospel account.

It is generally accepted that the Gospel of John was the latest of the four Gospels to be written. It is usually dated about AD 100. Most interpreters think it was probably written from Ephesus. Jerusalem fell and was totally destroyed in AD 70. So those who told the Gospel story later would have to write it somewhere else and would likely describe Jerusalem for the readers.

In this book the author will be referred to as the writer of the Gospel or the author of the Fourth Gospel or sometimes simply as John. But it will always be with the understanding that the question of authorship is not settled.

Audience

To whom was the Gospel of John written? This is not completely clear. Some think that it was written to Jewish Christians. Others find it addressed to Jews of the Dispersion, those Jews who lived outside the national homeland in Palestine. It could have been addressed to early Christians as they worshiped and witnessed. There are those who think that it was addressed to no one in particular but to the world at large.

The explanation of Jewish customs and Hebrew words supports the idea that it was written to some people who would not have been familiar with life in Israel. But it also leans heavily on Old Testament themes. Some have even identified it as the most Jewish of the Gospels, while others have found it to be oriented toward Greek philosophical concepts. William E. Hull observed in the *Broadman Bible Commentary* that the Gospel of John is a balanced attempt to preserve the Jewish heritage from the past, to clarify its Christian faith in the present, and to prepare for missionary responsibilities to the Gentiles in the future.

Thus looking at all three target groups—Jewish, Gentile, and Christian—and all three time frames—past, present, and future—the Gospel of John was sent out into the world to convince people that Jesus Christ was God's son, the Savior, and to challenge them to faith and commitment.

Approach

The approach or purpose of the Gospel of John, then, was evangelistic. The writer of the Fourth Gospel identified his purpose himself when he wrote: "These things are written that you may believe that Jesus is the Christ, the Son of God, and that believing you may have life in his name" (20:31).

The writer identified two concerns in this overall purpose. The first concern was that the recipients of the Gospel would come to the belief that Jesus was the Christ, the Messiah, who was the Son of God. To foster that belief he did not give the account of Jesus' birth but in the opening words of the Gospel identified Jesus, whom he called the Word, with God from all eternity. Jesus spoke repeatedly in the Gospel of having come from God and returning to God. The miracles, or signs, as John called them, were designed to prove conclusively that the power of God the Father resided in Jesus the Son. In his arrest, trial, crucifixion, and resurrection Jesus acted as a king. He was in control of the situation rather than being controlled by the tide of events. These things would bring about the belief that Jesus was indeed the Christ, God's son.

The second concern in the overall purpose was then to call for decision, to bring about the belief that through Jesus Christ a person could have new life, eternal life that would allow the individual to live forever in the forgiveness of his sin and the renewal of his life. Believing that Jesus was the Son of God, the Christ, then one could come to believe on him for salvation, new life. The purpose was to bring one to that kind of experiential belief on Jesus Christ that is complete commitment in faith to him.

But that is not the only concern in the Gospel of John. Other theological themes find their way into this Gospel.

Revelation is one of the theological themes John's Gospel emphasizes. Placing the coming of Christ into the world in the context of eternity, the Gospel shows how God made the disclosure of himself to humankind. Jesus related himself to the Father throughout the account. Through the reading of the Fourth Gospel one can not only know something of how God made himself known to the world but also of who the Father himself is. Insight into the character and concern of God are drawn from this Gospel.

The Christ who was from the very beginning of all eternity and who came into the world to reveal God and redeem persons left a group of folks behind. The church is a theme of interest to the writer of John's Gospel. This Gospel account shows the connection be tween the historical Jesus and the church. It is interested in the church continuing to carry out in the world the commission with which Jesus came into the world. The melting together of Jewish and Gentile believers into the one church of Jesus Christ is indicated. And, above all, the Spirit of Christ who permeates and empowers the church is made known.

The Holy Spirit is given a greater place in John's Gospel than in any other Gospel. Clement of Alexandria, an early church father, referred to the Gospel of John as the spiritual gospel. Not only is the Holy Spirit promised in John's Gospel, but also the work and ministry of the Holy Spirit with both Christians and church are outlined.

Attention is given to the Christ. From the study of this Gospel the preexistence of Christ is assured. The reality of the incarnation is emphasized. Jesus is such a real person that he hungered, tired, and grieved. One of the early heresies that may have been countered with this gospel was the heresy that saw Jesus as not a real human being but a being who just seemed to be human. That concept was refuted by John's Gospel where the incarnation of Jesus is affirmed. In Jesus Christ God became a man. And yet this man was so closely related to God that he could be identified with God. The claims of the Christ, the "I ams," show his nature. Christology is one of the focuses.

Analysis

The Gospel of John shows every evidence of being a very well-planned, balanced book. It begins with a prologue, follows with two sections, often called books, that show Jesus' ministry and his mission, and closes with an epilogue.

Notice how it is organized:

Prologue and Presentation—Chapter 1
Signs (often called the Book of Signs)—Chapters 2—12
Suffering (often called the Book of Passion)—Chapters 13—20
Epilogue—Chapter 21

The Gospel of John does not begin with a narrative of the birth of Jesus or even with his baptism or the inauguration of his public ministry. Instead, it begins with eternity. From the very beginning Jesus was. The prologue of 1:1-18 introduces him in poetic form. Then in prose form Jesus is presented to the world he has come to save. These first presentations were to people of Israel who would follow him. From them would come the New Israel of faith.

What the other Gospels identify as miracles, the writer of John's Gospel called signs. A sign points beyond itself. The author carefully selected seven signs to point beyond themselves to God and to explain the character of the Christ. These signs were often followed by discourses which spelled out more completely the significance of the sign. For instance, in John 6 Jesus multiplied the loaves and fishes and fed five thousand men, a miracle recorded by all four Gospels. Then in the discourse that followed he explained that he was the Bread of life.

Another interesting feature of John's Gospel is that he seems at times to be talking on two levels. There is an immediate, obvious level but also a deeper, more spiritual meaning to the statement. Nicodemus, for instance, took the statement about being born again on the literal level while Jesus had reference to a deeper spiritual meaning, being born from above by faith.

The writer of the Fourth Gospel was also fond of contrasts. Throughout the Gospel are found contrasts such as light and darkness, love and hate, life and death, belief and unbelief. Persons are faced with a choice. The contrasts between what they are and what they can be, where they are and where they can be are clearly drawn.

The public ministry of Jesus closed with chapter 12. The remainder of the book (ch. 13—20) deals with the last week of his life, culminating in his crucifixion and climaxed by his resurrection. Chapters 13—17 contain the farewell discourses. They reveal the inner mind of Jesus and his teaching to his disciples more clearly than any other material in the Gospels.

Many interpreters consider the epilogue, chapter 21, to have been written later than the rest of the Gospel and by another hand. The arguments either way are not conclusive. While it may have been written later it appears to be an integral part of the book as it has been preserved. Without that epilogue the book would not be as balanced and well-rounded.

From early times people tried to account for the differences in John's Gospel by supposing that it was meant to supplement the Synoptic Gospels. If the book was written later, as most people think, the writer of the Fourth Gospel probably was familiar with one or all three of the Synoptic Gospels. It seems better to assume that the Gospel of John was written in its own style to accomplish its own purpose rather than to consider it in relationship to the Synoptic Gospels. It is capable of standing on its own and of being received on its own merits.

This study is an exposition of the text of the Gospel of John. The Fourth Gospel is not treated in relationship to the Synoptic Gospels other than by occasional references to them for comparison and clarification. In keeping with the intent of this series, technical problems are not examined.

As with the original text of John's Gospel, this work is sent out with the prayer that those reading it will believe that Jesus is the Christ and that believing on him they might have life in his name.

Prologue

1:1-18

The prologue to John's Gospel is more than a preface. In these eighteen verses he introduced and explained all that is found in the remainder of the Gospel. In a great piece of music the composer often begins by stating the themes he is going to work out and elaborate in the course of the whole work. John did that in the prologue. The themes found running throughout the Gospel are introduced in the prologue.

The Word (1:1)

To express the eternality and the preexistence of Jesus Christ, John employed an expression that would speak to all the people who would read his Gospel. Rather than positioning Jesus in the lineage of the king, as did Matthew, or in the time of the Roman rulers, as did Luke, John declared Christ's existence from the very beginning.

In words that are reminiscent of the opening words of the Bible in Genesis, John asserted that "In the beginning was the Word" (v. 1). The Word was with God but was also distinct from God. The Word was not just identified with God: he was identical with God.

For all the first readers who would pick up this Gospel, the expression "Word" had meaning. To the Jews, the word of God meant power. The prophets spoke the word of the Lord. When God spoke, the world came into being (Gen. 1:1). The word of God had purpose (Isa. 55:11). The word of God could burn like fire or shatter like a hammer (Jer. 23:29). To the Greeks, the word meant principle. It was the rational principle, the rational mind, that ruled the universe. To the Christians, the Word meant proclamation. The preaching of the gospel was a "ministry of the word" (Acts 6:4). But above all, the Word was personal. God had a word to say to humankind, something to communicate to his creation. Any communication becomes more real when it is personal. The Word was a person. That person was Jesus Christ.

The Word was always present with God. In fact, the Word was God. And this Word was God's supreme communication.

The Word and Creation (1:2-5)

The Word which God used to communicate was a comprehensive Word. It was related to God in that it was identical to God. From the very beginning, the Word existed with God.

The Word was related to the world by creation. God was always known by his creativity and his redemption. In the Word both creation and redemption were expressed. All things were made by the Word as the agent of creation. Nothing was omitted from the creative activity of the Word.

Redemption was known also through the Word. For "in him was life" (v. 4). Thus the comprehensive Word also related to humankind. Through the Word who brought life, persons can be redeemed and can know life in its full and true meaning. Later in this Gospel the Word himself explained the life that he brought: "I came that they may have life, and have it abundantly" (10:10). To hopeless people, the Word brought meaningful life.

But the revelation of God is also known by the Word in his relationship to humankind. Not only did he bring life, he also brought light.

The Word brought light into the world. Light about darkened

ideas concerning sin, self, and salvation was brought by the Word. The light of God's love shines upon persons through Jesus Christ. Twice in the Fourth Gospel Jesus made the claim for himself, "I am the light of the world" (8:12; 9:5).

Notice something about that light. It shines in the darkness of the world around it, and the darkness can never put it out. The light always dispels darkness; the darkness never extinguishes the light.

Jesus Christ came into the world to reveal God and to redeem persons. John expresses those two purposes with light and life.

The Word and the World (1:6-18)

The Word came into the world as a person. The witness to that Word was given by a person. A man was sent by God. John was sent into the world by God's commission as a witness to the Light. Also a child of promise, John the Baptist was the forerunner of Jesus. He was to give testimony to the Word which brought light to the darkened world. The purpose was that "all might believe through him" (v. 7).

Some of John the Baptist's followers had trouble transferring loyalty from John to Jesus. In order to show that John's purpose was witness whereas Jesus' purpose was light and life, the author carefully distinguishes John the Baptist from Jesus. John was to bear witness to the Light; he was not the Light (v. 8).

The Word, which was Jesus Christ, would bring light to all persons. The purpose of God was inclusive; no one was excluded who did not exclude himself.

The Word, who was the agent of creation, came to the world that he had created and to the people who were especially prepared for his coming. The response was generally negative: rejection. But rejection was not the total response. There was also a positive response by some: acceptance. To those who accepted the life and light that the Word brought into the world by receiving him through faith, God gave the privilege of becoming his children. For John, the verb form "believe" (v. 12, KJV) is used rather than the noun form "faith." A verb expresses action. Those who acted out their belief were made children of God by faith. This new creation was not a human act nor did it come from human will. It was a work of God's grace.

The Word took on personality. The Word became a person. For the first time in his prologue John gave a name to the Word, a name known and understood: Jesus Christ (v. 17). There is a continuity between the preexistent creative Word of God and the Word as he became flesh and was known as a human personality. This Word was not remote from human beings. He lived among persons. The word "dwelt" literally means "tabernacled" (v. 14). The tabernacle was a tent used for worship by the Hebrews on their wilderness wanderings. God pitched his tent among persons in Jesus Christ.

From the presence of Christ on the earth, people can know both grace and truth. Grace is the unmerited favor of God. Truth shows that God is predictable, consistent, trustworthy. These characteristics of God were personified in the Word.

Through the Word that became person, the glory of God could be experienced. Glory also goes back to the tabernacle in the wilderness where the glory of God dwelt. Glory means literally the presence. The presence of God which is his glory is known and experienced through the Word.

Before the Word could be exalted he had to be limited. When the Word became flesh it was the only-one-of-his-kind Son of God. He was limited by time, temperament, and temporariness as a human. But in him was seen the fullness of God, the full making known of God to persons. And that brought his exaltation as the Son of God.

The Word-became-flesh was evaluated both in terms of John the Baptist, his witness, and the Jewish hero, Moses. Although John the Baptist was before Jesus in terms of time since he was older, Jesus was before John in terms of purpose. John was the forerunner. Jesus was the one to whom he pointed. The Christ was also before John through preexistence.

Moses was the great hero of the Jewish faith because the Law had been revealed through him and redemption from slavery in Egypt had been achieved through him. But Jesus brought grace and truth (v. 14). His revelation of God was supreme, and his redemption was complete. The law can show the need for deliverance from sin; only the grace and truth expressed by Jesus can deliver from sin. The truth that God has been consistently active in redemption is made known through his grace in Jesus Christ. And this grace is received "one blessing after another" (1:16, GNB).

No human being has ever actually seen God. But the Word who had an intimate relationship with him has declared him to humans. "Declared" (v. 18, KJV) is literally "exegeted." When a passage of Scripture is exegeted, it is explained precisely and clearly. This Jesus has done. The unseen God, the Father, is explained by the seen Jesus, the Son. A new creative and redemptive act was begun through the Word who became a person.

Presentation

1:19-51

By John (1:19-34)

Moving from poetry to prose, the witness of John the Baptist to Jesus is made specific. The prologue had presented Jesus Christ as preexistent Word who had become human in a person, Jesus of Nazareth. Now that person is presented to the world.

A committee of the Jews composed of priests, Levites, and Pharisees called on John. This group of Jewish leaders usually opposed Jesus. They had a question for John: "Who are you?" (v. 19). In response to their question of his identity, John the Baptist made a threefold denial that he was the Christ. Christ was a title rather than a name; it indicated the anointed one of God, the Messiah. John's first witness was negative.

If he were not the Christ, was he then Elijah? The Jewish people thought that Elijah who had been taken directly to heaven would reappear prior to the coming of the Messiah. John was not Elijah.

Then they thought that perhaps John was the prophet predicted in Deuteronomy 18:15 who would also precede the Messiah. That designation John also denied.

Further pressed for a definite identification of himself, John the Baptist answered in the words of Isaiah 40:3. He was a voice that was crying in the wilderness. His purpose was to prepare a straight and smooth roadway for the passage of the Lord as one would for a king in his travels.

The next question had to do with John's activity. If he were not the Christ, why was he baptizing even Jews as though they needed to be cleansed as did Gentiles? Baptism was not unknown to the Jews. Gentiles who converted to Judaism had to be baptized as a symbol of cleansing from their Gentile practices. John's baptism was a baptism that symbolized repentance. They could not understand why Jews would need cleansing as though they, too, were sinners. John's reply indicated that his baptism was in water, a symbol of the cleansing of repentance, but the one to whom he pointed would immerse people in the power of the Spirit of God. They did not know this one. Yet John did not even consider himself worthy of performing the slave's function of untying his sandal thong, so great was he.

This questioning by the committee took place near the Jordan River where John was preaching and baptizing at an unknown spot variously identified as Bethabara (KJV) and Bethany (RSV, v. 28).

The next day, John the Baptist gave a positive witness to Jesus. As John's denial that he himself was the Christ was threefold, so his witness to the Christ was threefold.

Upon seeing Jesus he announced: "Behold, the Lamb of God, who takes away the sin of the world!" (v. 29). That statement identified Jesus with the Old Testament concept of the sacrificial lamb and also stated his purpose to be the redemption of all humankind.

John further identified Jesus as the one who had come after him in time but who actually was before him both by preexistence and by purpose (v. 30). While it could mean that John had not previously met Jesus, he probably meant that he had not known Jesus as the Christ until his baptism.

The baptism of Jesus by John the Baptist is not recorded in John's Gospel, but the descent of the Holy Spirit upon him in the form of a dove is mentioned. This was the sign that would identify the Christ to John. And this John saw in Jesus.

John's baptism was in water signifying repentance. Jesus would immerse the people in the power of the Holy Spirit. Of this John gave witness when he presented Jesus as the Son of God.

To Disciples (1:35-51)

Andrew and Another (1:35-42)

From the general witness of John to Jesus, the Gospel account turns to the specific witness to two of the disciples or learners of John the Baptist. True to his purpose as the forerunner, John sought to transfer the loyalty of his followers to the Christ.

One of these disciples introduced to Jesus by the repetition of the designation "the Lamb of God" was Andrew (v. 40). While the other disciple is not named, it is strongly surmised that he was the apostle John. The account bears many marks of an eyewitness—the attention given to the time sequence, for instance.

As they followed Jesus, he inquired of them what they wanted. When they answered, "Rabbi, . . . where are you staying?" (v. 38), they were doing more than asking his address. By the term *Rabbi* they were addressing him as a teacher. The inquiry indicated that they wanted to spend time with him in discussion. Responding to their query, Jesus invited them to come and see where he stayed and what he taught. They went with him.

After spending the evening with Jesus, Andrew found his brother Simon and gave a startling announcement: "We have found the Messiah" (v. 41). As an indication that the Gospel of John was intended for Gentile as well as Jewish readers, the writer explained that "Messiah" was in the Hebrew as "Christ" was in the Greek, the term for the Anointed One of God. There is a possibility from the construction that the passage indicates that Andrew found his brother Simon before the other unnamed disciple found his brother. Likely, it means that the first thing Andrew did was to find his brother to share with him what he had discovered—the Christ.

In a searching look Jesus indicated that he knew that he was Simon, John's son. But he would have a new name, a nickname meaning "rock." The Christ could give him a new name, for he would have a new character. Simon would be understood in terms of his future.

Philip and Nathaniel (1:43-51)

The previous activity had been in Judea. On the day following the encounter with Simon Peter, Jesus went from Judea to Galilee. Galilee was to the north and was known as "Galilee of the Gentiles" because of the concentration of Gentiles in its population. Much of Jesus' ministry was in Galilee.

Jesus took the initiative in calling Philip, who was from Bethsaida, the hometown of Andrew and Peter, to follow him. The invitation was simple: "Follow me" (v. 43). Following Jesus is the nature of Christian discipleship. In obedience, one relates to the Savior through faith and follows him throughout life.

True to the nature of the Christian faith, Philip shared his experience with Christ with another. To Nathaniel he announced that the one to whom the whole Scripture gave witness had been found. He identified him as Jesus of Nazareth who was known as the son of Joseph.

Nathaniel's reply, "Can anything good come out of Nazareth?" (v. 46), may have reflected provincial prejudice, a proverb that put down Nazareth, or the judgment of a student of Scripture who had found prophetic references neither to Nazareth nor a son of Joseph. But Philip's invitation was the invitation to discipleship: "Come and see" (v. 46). Discipleship must be personally experienced.

Upon seeing Nathaniel, Jesus immediately assessed him as an Israelite of transparent character, one in whom there was no guile. This astonished Nathaniel who asked how he could have known that. Jesus answered that he had seen him under his fig tree before Philip had called him. While he may actually have been at home under a fig tree, the reference also reflects an Old Testament figure of the ideal setting for the study of the law.

Nathaniel turned from skepticism to faith. Rather than the derisive term of the son of Joseph, he addressed Jesus as the Son of God who was the king of Israel.

Jesus predicted that Nathaniel who had come to faith by such a simple revelation would see even greater things. Why, it would be as though the very heavens would open and God's truth would be communicated from heaven to earth. Rather than the ladder in Jacob's Old Testament vision, the Son of Man, Christ himself, would be the medium of revelation of heavenly things to earthly folk.

The term "Son of man" (v. 51) is a messianic term of Old Testament background. It did more than identify Jesus as a human; it is a term that points to his heavenly origins and glory and also of his lowliness and humility in showing God to others through his suffering. It is the term used most often by Jesus to identify himself.

At least three themes have been identified by interpreters in the prologue of the Gospel and the presentation of Jesus. One theme has to do with the introduction of Jesus to the old Israel and his continuity with it as he began to form the new Israel. Another idea finds significance in the numbering of the days. Tying these days in chapter 1 with the days mentioned in chapter 2, these interpreters would find a creative week similar to the week of creation in Genesis. This is God's new creation in Jesus Christ. Others have found in the questioning of John the Baptist by the Jewish committee an indication of the trial through which Jesus went all of his ministry, culminating in the guilty verdict that brought about his crucifixion. Whichever or whatever theme is found, Christ has been introduced to the world he came to save.

Signs

2:1 to 12:50

Following the prologue to the Fourth Gospel the first major division concerns the signs that Jesus used to point beyond himself to a truth about God. In doing this, Jesus was making himself known to the old Israel prior to the formation of the new Israel. These eleven chapters have to do with the public ministry of Jesus, whereas the chapters that follow center more in the private ministry of Jesus with his followers.

In the Gospel of John the word *sign* is used rather than *miracle*. A sign points beyond itself to a major truth about God made known through Jesus Christ. A miracle is never a miracle for its own sake. As used by the writer of John's Gospel the miracle is always a sign that points beyond the event to a greater truth.

Seven signs are found in the Gospel of John. That number is no accident. In the symbolism of numbers, seven is the number for completeness. In these seven signs, selected from the many things done by Jesus (20:30-31), is the completeness of the revelation of God through Jesus Christ. Each of the signs tells something about the nature and ministry of Jesus. Together they tell the complete story. They are signs of the Savior that compel belief.

Revelation (2:1 to 4:54)

In quick succession of events Jesus is made known to the world.

Turning Water into Wine: A New Joy (2:1-12)

Jesus' first miracle or sign was the climax of the week of revelation in which Jesus was introduced to the world. It took place in Cana in the area of Galilee. Cana was probably about eight or nine miles north of Nazareth which was also in Galilee.

A wedding feast was a festive occasion that could last as long as a week. With marriages arranged in advance and life often a troublesome toil, the wedding feast could well be the high point in a couple's life. To this feast came Mary, the mother of Jesus, who could have been a relative of the couple, along with Jesus and those who had begun to follow him.

During the course of the festivities the wine ran out. Not only would this be an embarrassing situation for the family, it could also expose them to legal liability. Certainly, the couple would have their joyous occasion ruined both at the moment and in memory.

Mary informed Jesus that the wine was exhausted. His answer to her (v. 4) is not really as curt and indifferent as it sounds to us. "Woman" is a term of respect, much like "lady." The second part of the reply asked what that had to do with them. It really made no difference in the relationship between Jesus and Mary. And by his statement that "My hour has not yet come" Jesus was saying that the time had not yet come for his manifestation and glorification. Throughout the Gospel of John the "hour" of Jesus was used to refer to his crucifixion and resurrection by which his purpose of redemption and glorification was realized.

Mary, who had remembered all the things concerning the announcement and the birth of Jesus and had pondered them in her heart (Luke 2:19), likely thought this was a good time to make Jesus known. But Jesus would not be pushed into action. The time had not yet come to make known his messianic mission. Nevertheless, Mary told the servants to do what Jesus told them.

Refusing to be pushed into action, Jesus voluntarily acted.

Standing nearby were six large stone waterpots that held twenty to thirty gallons of water. They were used for Jewish ceremonial purposes. These waterpots supplied the water that was used in ritual washings before and after meals or after traveling. Jesus had them filled to the brim, which would indicate that there was nothing but water in them. Then he told the servants to draw out the water and take it to the steward of the feast. It is not clear at what point the water was changed to wine, when it was drawn out or when it was served up. Neither is it really clear as to where water-turned-wine was drawn, whether from the waterpots or from the well. John was not as interested in those details of the miracle as in the meaning of the event.

When taken to the steward, who was rather like a master of ceremonies, he remarked that the quality of that wine was better than before and also rather joshed the bridegroom for keeping the best until the last. Most of the people present seemed to be unaware that any extraordinary event had occurred. The bridegroom and the steward did not seem to know; the servants and the disciples did not seem to know.

The reason for this sign was more than an attempt to relieve an embarrassing situation; it was also more than just an incidental reminder that it was the first miracle Jesus performed. A result of the miracle was that the disciples believed on Jesus (v. 11). It was a major step in the self-revelation of Jesus to those who would follow him.

In the symbolic use of numbers, seven is a number of completion. The number six indicates something just short of completion. Six waterpots were used. These waterpots were connected to the Jewish ritual observances. Later Jesus would remark that no one put new wine in old wineskins else the new wine burst out of the old wineskins (Mark 2:22). The knowledge they had of God and their relationship to God through the Jewish law was incomplete. One thing was needed to make it complete. That Jesus supplied. With Jesus there is a full and complete revelation of God. People can now know God fully. Also, God's supply is in abundance; there is little likelihood that they would have exhausted 120 to 180 gallons of wine, especially if it were watered down as the custom was. And Jesus brings new joy into life. When life has gone stale, dull, and flat, Jesus can introduce a new note of joy, sparkle, and vitality.

After this event Jesus journeyed to Capernaum, also in Galilee. There according to the Synoptic Gospels he had an extensive ministry. At this point, his family was apparently still supportive of him. Later they would reject him.

Cleansing the Temple: A New Worship (2:13-25)

After an unspecified time in Capernaum Jesus went to Jerusalem for the Feast of the Passover. John's calling it "the Passover of the Jews" (v. 13) is an indication that his Gospel was written primarily for Gentile readers. This is one of three Passovers directly mentioned in the Fourth Gospel (2:13; 6:4; 13:1), which helps to set the duration of Jesus' ministry as about three years.

When Jesus arrived at the Temple he found them selling oxen, sheep, and pigeons there, as well as changing money. The "temple" usually refers to the whole Temple complex which was composed of several courts. This was probably in the outer court, the Court of the Gentiles. That was as far in the Temple as a Gentile could go.

Many of the people who came to the Passover had come long distances. The selling of the animals used for sacrifice was a convenience. They would not have to bring the sacrificial animals with them. And animals that may have started out in good shape may not have been without blemish by the time they reached Jerusalem and the Temple. In addition, only a certain coin was acceptable for payment of the Temple tax. The money changers changed the coins that people had brought from many places to the coins authorized for use in the Temple.

When Jesus saw this commerce taking place in the one place in the Temple where compassion for the Gentiles should have been shown, he was incensed. Taking a whip of cords made from cords that had tied things together or even from reeds or shucks, he chased them from the Temple court (v. 15). Chasing oxen, sheep, pigeons, and traders before him, turning over the tables of the money changers, and pouring out their coins, he charged them with making the house of God a house of trade. Notice that he called it "my Father's house" (v. 16), thus indicating something of his unique sonship. The disciples recalled a Scripture verse from Psalms 69:9 as they saw his zeal in cleansing the Temple.

The Synoptic Gospels also record a cleansing of the Temple by Jesus. They, however, put it in the last week of Jesus' life as one of the things leading up to his death. John has put it at the beginning of Jesus' ministry, as his first public act.

There may well have been two such acts on Jesus' part. He may have expressed his rage at what he saw at his first Passover and then again toward the end of his ministry. Or each of the Gospel writers could have placed the event according to the emphasis he wanted to place on it. The Synoptic Gospels emphasize that it was one of the things that sealed Jesus' doom. John, however, by placing it at the beginning of Jesus' ministry would indicate that there was always tension between Jesus and the Jewish leaders. From the very start he had thrown down a gauntlet and issued a challenge to them. At all points in his public ministry Jesus was on trial before them—which he turned to use as a trial of them before God's truth.

Obviously upset by what he had done, the Jewish leaders, who would have been the Sadducees who had control of the Temple, demanded to know his authority for such an action. They wanted a sign to show where he had the power to disrupt their dealings. Interestingly enough, they did not ask why he had done it, only by what authority he had done it (v. 18).

Jesus' answer was a rather cryptic remark about destroying the Temple and he would rebuild it in three days (v. 19). This would later be used against him in his trial (Mark 14:58). His questioners took him literally and answered that the Temple had been in the process of being rebuilt since Herod had undertaken the project forty-six years before. It would not be completed until AD 64. How could he rebuild it in three days?

Often in John's Gospel statements of Jesus have double meaning. That is true here. In an editorial explanation, the Gospel writer (vv. 21-22) explained that his primary reference was to Jesus' resurrection from the dead. Jesus would never do a miracle just to impress someone or to prove a point. To their demand for a sign to show his authority Jesus gave a statement that would have its ultimate meaning made clear in his resurrection from the dead. Those who were closest to him did not catch the reference at the time. Only after the event of the resurrection could they look back at that statement and realize what Jesus had in mind. Jesus took their literal reply to his statement and used it to drive home a spiritual truth.

When Jesus cleansed the Temple he introduced a new kind of

worship. They had substituted convenience for compassion and sacrifice for submission to the will of God. Jesus showed them that the Father demanded sincerity and truth in worship. In essence they had destroyed the Temple by their perversion of worship. But when the Temple which was Christ's body would be destroyed by their crucifixion of him, after three days it would be resurrected to form the body of Christ, the church, by which God would be truly known. The sign they demanded could only be known after Jesus' hour had fully come through his death and resurrection. All persons in the world could know God through the resurrected Christ without the limitations imposed by the Temple which they were protecting.

Some of the people who were at the Passover feast in Jerusalem believed on Jesus (v. 23). But these were superficial believers who believed on him because of the signs that they had seen him do. Impressed by the signs, they believed.

But even though they believed in him, Jesus did not believe in them. Jesus refused to commit himself to them (v. 24). Knowing human nature as he did, he knew that their belief was a superficial belief that would not last. He did not need anyone to interpret to him the commitment of persons; he knew the human heart too well for that.

Entering the Kingdom of God: A New Birth (3:1-21)

Even though Jesus did not trust himself to those superficial believers at the Passover, there was one to whom he did trust himself: Nicodemus. (Nicodemus is also mentioned in 7:50 and 19:39.)

Nicodemus was the man who had everything: power, prestige, and position. Yet he came in the night to speak with Jesus. He wanted more than he had; and he wanted to know more about what Jesus was teaching. In the Fourth Gospel Jesus is not only made known through signs but also through discourses. This is the first discourse.

The Pharisees were the group of the Jews who were most interested in following the Law precisely. They were actually the best examples of first-century Judaism. Religion was a serious matter to them. The Sanhedrin was a council of seventy elders. It was the highest court among the Jews. The expression "a ruler of the

Jews" (v. 1) is usually understood to mean that Nicodemus was a member of that court. Jesus called him "a teacher of Israel" (v. 10), which is taken to mean a trained theologian. If anyone could have right standing with God by being a Jew, Nicodemus would have been that one.

Since Nicodemus was representative of the ruling people, some have assumed that he came as a representative rather than as an individual inquirer. Probably he came as an individual with an interest in Jesus and his teaching. John then used him as representative of those who best represented Judaism. Even they needed a birth from above to be a part of God's kingdom.

Why did Nicodemus come to see Jesus at night? The answers vary. Some think it was because of fear, embarrassment, or the desire not to be seen. Others think it was because night was when the Law was usually studied and discussed, because of schedule, or as a symbol of his darkened thinking. Likely the evening hours were the best time for two men who were both often in crowds to have a leisurely and uninterrupted conversation.

Nicodemus opened the conversation with a compliment. Calling him "Rabbi" or teacher even though he knew that Jesus was not formally trained, he also made the observation that God must be with him because of what he had done. The signs from God had been recognized. Cutting through the compliment Jesus got to the heart of the matter: no one could even see the kingdom of God unless he was born from above (v. 3).

This startling statement hit at the center of the belief of people like Nicodemus. They took great pride in their physical descent from Abraham. They were serious about keeping the Law. They gave great study to the kingdom of God and, indeed, lived in expectation of its breaking into human history. Now Jesus had said that they could not even see the kingdom of God, to say nothing of entering the kingdom of God, without a new birth. The term "born anew" can also mean "born from above," which would indicate a birth from God.

Interpreting the statement literally, Nicodemus asked, perhaps rather wistfully, how a grown person could be born again. Obviously, his mother could not bear him again physically (v. 4). Taking the literal answer, Jesus gave to it a spiritual interpretation in the way that John's Gospel often uses a statement on two levels.

There is a distinct difference between a physical birth and a spiritual birth (v. 6). Jesus was not talking here about a physical birth; he had reference to a spiritual birth. Rephrasing his statement he asserted that unless one was born of both water and Spirit he could not enter the kingdom of God (v. 5).

There has been a continuing discussion of the meaning of "water and the Spirit." The meaning of Spirit is quite clear. It is a reference to the spiritual rebirth, regeneration, brought about by the activity of the Holy Spirit in a human life. But what about water? Some have thought it was another reference to physical birth, either through the water that accompanied a physical birth or the semen that brought about conception. Others have found in it a reference to baptism and have taught baptismal regeneration from it. Still others find in it an indication of the cleansing or purification that must accompany salvation. Since Nicodemus would have been familiar with the baptism of John the Baptist, which was a baptism signifying repentance, it is possible that this is the primary reference. If this is correct, Jesus would have told him that unless he had repentance as represented by John's baptism and the activity of the Holy Spirit which brought new life he could not enter the kingdom of God.

Nicodemus should not have thought this strange. After all, he never saw the wind nor did he know either the source or the destination of the wind. But Nicodemus knew the wind had been blowing by its effects. The same word translates both "wind" and "spirit" in the original language in which the Gospel was written. In this play on words Jesus showed Nicodemus that he could tell the reality of the new birth, that birth from above, by its results in a life (v. 8).

For the second time Nicodemus asked the question, "How can this be?" (v. 9). Jesus gently chided him when he asked how he could be a teacher of Israel, a trained theologian, and not understand those things. He had told him about earthly things—water, wind, and birth which he used as analogies—and he had not believed them. Would he believe the heavenly things—the marvelous, mysterious moving of the Holy Spirit in human life?

Testimony is always based on what is known (v. 11). Jesus was bearing witness to what he knew. No one had ever gone from earth to heaven to learn the spiritual truths. That kind of information had to come from the other direction, from heaven to earth. The only one who had come from heaven to earth to share the heavenly truths was the Son of man. Without making it specific, Jesus was the Son of man. Son of man was a messianic term which Jesus often used to refer to himself because it did not carry with it all the interpretations that were attached to the term *Messiah*.

Then Jesus used an incident from Hebrew history to instruct further the teacher of Israel. He reminded him of the time in the wilderness when the people were bitten by snakes. A brass snake was formed and put on a stick and lifted up in the camp. Only those who looked at the snake could be healed (Num. 21:9). So the Son of man must be lifted up. This is a veiled reference to the cross by which Jesus was both literally lifted up and also glorified. That was his hour. Those who believe in Jesus, that exalted Son of man, are the ones who will have eternal life.

"Believe" means more than intellectual assent. It means the total commitment of the life in faith. "Eternal life" has more of a reference to quality than quantity. While quantity is involved, a life that never ends, the primary consideration is to the life of eternal quality, a life fit for eternity. That kind of life comes only through faith in Jesus the Christ.

So in answer to the rather wistful question of the older man, "How can a man be born when he is old?" (v. 4)—and his later question, "How can these things be?" (v. 9, KJV)—Jesus taught that it is through faith in him. Both the questions are answered by belief. One can be born anew through faith in Christ. The Christ is the very one, the only one, who has come from heaven to earth to teach heavenly truths and to make it possible for people to have an eternity with God in heaven. Jesus had led Nicodemus from the darkness to the light.

It is sometimes difficult to tell in the Fourth Gospel where the words of Jesus leave off and the words of the writer take up. This is one of these places. Most interpreters think that the discourse with Nicodemus ended with verse 15 and that verses 16 through 21 were the discussion of the Gospel writer.

John 3:16 is certainly one of the clearest interpretive statements in the Scripture. Martin Luther referred to it as the gospel in miniature. It was because God loved the whole world, and not just the Jews, that Jesus came into the world. Jesus, the only begotten son of God, the only-one-of-his-kind Son of God, was given for the sin of the world. Jesus had a unique kind of sonship with God not shared by any other. His death did not occur because the situation had gotten out of control or because there was a division between the love of the Son and the wrath of the Father. The death of Jesus for our sins was prompted by the depth of God's love for us. It was the supreme gift of God's grace to us. Those who believe on Jesus are the ones who receive eternal life. There is no perishing when one turns in faith to Christ.

The primary purpose of the coming of Jesus into the world was not to bring judgment and condemnation into the world. His primary purpose was to bring salvation and deliverance to the world. Nevertheless, there is a division, a judgment, between those who believe in him and those who do not. The basis of judgment is whether one believes in Jesus, accepts him or rejects him (v. 19). Those who accept him are not condemned; those who reject him have already been condemned on the basis of their rejection of the Christ, the light of the world.

The light of God's love and grace has come into the world in Jesus (v. 19). But some people have rejected that light, loving darkness rather than light. They love darkness because their actions are of the darkness, evil, and they do not want them exposed to the light (v. 20). But the persons whose lives are characterized by the truth are drawn to the light. God's light of love and grace always exposes that which is dark and evil while attracting that which is true and pure.

Clarifying the Ministry of John: A New Master (3:22-36)

At some unspecified time following the visit between Jesus and Nicodemus, Jesus and his disciples left Jerusalem and went into the surrounding area of Judea. There he preached his message of repentance and faith and baptized those who responded. John 4:2 corrects the impression that Jesus had actually administered the baptisms himself with the notation that the disciples actually did the act of baptizing.

This is an early ministry in Judea that is not mentioned by the Synoptic Gospels. At the same time, John the Baptist had continued his ministry, moving a little farther north. The exact site of "Aenon near Salim" (v. 23) is not known. While the ministries of Jesus and John overlapped they did not compete. People were still responding to the ministry of John the Baptist; those were baptized with a baptism that indicated repentance, not Christian baptism, in the abundant water of the area where he preached. This, of course, was prior to his imprisonment by Herod. This brief statement (v. 24) is the only reference in the Fourth Gospel to the imprisonment of John the Baptist.

There were some other Jews who were practicing a rite of purification which may have also involved some form of baptism. One of these and the followers of John the Baptist got into an argument over the matter of ceremonial purification. Likely they were discussing the relative merits of the baptism of John and the baptism of Jesus.

Carrying the argument back to John, they reported that Jesus, the very one who had been with him beyond the Jordan (which could indicate an unrecorded joint ministry), was baptizing. John had baptized him and had borne witness to him. And not only that, people were going in throngs to hear him. The "all" (v. 26) would not mean literally every single person but great groups, or all who turned out. Obviously, the disciples of John were concerned about the turn of events. They felt that John's place had been usurped by Jesus.

John's gracious answer clarified the relationship between him and Jesus. Each person has the place and responsibility that God has given him (v. 27). John had his place; Jesus had his place. Both were given by God. John reminded them that he had given witness to Jesus himself. He had never claimed to be the Christ, God's promised, the Anointed One. He was sent as a forerunner of the Christ, to prepare the way. That he had done. Using the analogy of the friend of the bridegroom, or the best man, John found his joy in introducing Jesus to Israel. The friend of the groom had the responsibility of presenting the bride to the bridegroom. He rejoiced in the bridal couple's joy. Jesus must increase; John would decrease. Jesus would have to be recognized and followed. John would recede into the background. There was a new master: the Christ sent from God.

This clarification was intended not only to answer the question of John's followers at the time but also to answer the controversy that might arise between the followers of John and the church. Jesus was the new master. John had pointed the way.

Drifting past the incident to an interpretation, the writer of the Fourth Gospel again gives an explanation about Jesus (v. 31). The one who comes from heaven—above—is above the one who is earthbound. Jesus, who was identified in the prologue as the preexistent Son of God, had come from heaven to earth. The witness that he would give to God was the testimony of what he had experienced. Rather than a secondhand account, it was a witness of what he had seen and heard. What he witnessed was that God is true.

The Son has the full measure of the Holy Spirit. The words that he speaks are the words of God. Into his hands the Father has given all things. Not everyone receives the testimony that the Son has given. These persons face judgment. The basis of judgment is the Son himself and whether they receive or reject him.

The person who believes the Son has eternal life. This is the life that is eternal in quality. It is life in its fullness. But the opposite side of that is that the one who does not believe in the Son does not see, or enter into, life. The contrasts are between believing on Jesus Christ as personal Savior or rejecting him, between life and death, between obedience and disobedience. Obedience is equated with belief. The person who believes in Jesus will obey Jesus and will follow him into life.

The result of rejection is that the wrath of God will abide, will continue to stay, on that person who rejects Christ. The wrath of God is never arbitrary and capricious. It is the constant, continuous opposition of God against sin.

The issue is clearly presented. Each person is personally confronted by the Christ and personally responsible for a decision. The way of life or the way of death opens up. The way of life is entered by believing in Jesus. So there also opens up the possibility of obedience or disobedience, acceptance or rejection. The result of that decision is either life in fellowship with God or wrath expressed by God. What one does with Jesus makes a difference. The new Master leads to new life.

Encountering the Samaritan Woman: A New Inclusiveness (4:1-42)

The success of the ministry of Jesus in Judea was not without cost. The attention of the Pharisees, the leading group of Jewish leaders, was drawn to the number of followers that Jesus and his disciples were baptizing. (The writer took the opportunity in 4:2 to correct the statement in 3:22 that Jesus had baptized persons; the disciples actually had administered the baptisms.) Because of that attention and the opposition that it engendered, Jesus left Judea to return to Galilee.

His journey from Judea to Galilee took Jesus through Samaria. The fact that Jesus "had to pass through Samaria" (v. 4) was not due to geographical necessity but to divine purpose. Jesus could have crossed the Jordan River, traveled north toward Galilee, and then crossed the Jordan River again to enter Galilee just below the Sea of Galilee. Most Jews did circumvent Samaria that way. But due to divine purpose Jesus had to go to Galilee by the more direct route through Samaria.

When the Northern Kingdom was defeated by Assyria most of the people were carried away in captivity. Only the poorest people were left. In turn, the Assyrians imported captive people from other areas. They not only intermarried with the people who were there but also brought the worship of their gods with them. In time, the worship of the false gods died out, but their worship of God had some peculiarities. They accepted only the Pentateuch, the first five books of the Bible. They worshiped only at their own temple on Mount Gerizim. And they had fierce animosity toward the Jews. This was due, in part, to the fact that when the Jews of the Southern Kingdom returned from the Babylonian captivity the Samaritans offered to help in the rebuilding of the Temple. The Jews spurned the help of the Samaritans. Then when the Temple was rebuilt the Jews insisted that worship be centered in Jerusalem. This the Samaritans refused to do. The matter was made worse when the Jews burned the Samaritans' Temple in 128 BC. Because of racial impurity and religious irregularities the Samaritans were considered by the Jews to be inferior folk. The Samaritans returned the hate.

On his journey to Galilee Jesus reached Jacob's well at Sychar about noon. Tired from the trip, he sat on the edge of the well while his disciples went into the town to buy food. While sitting there resting, a Samaritan woman came to the well to draw water. Normally, women got the water in the cool of the morning or the early evening. Normally, also, the women would come together to the well, making it an opportunity for socializing. There can only be speculation about why this woman came alone at noon to the well for water. In the later revelation of her character by Jesus there is the hint that it was a matter of convenience and self-protection that brought her there alone. She would not have to face the comments of the other women. Having nothing to use to draw water Jesus asked the woman for a drink (v. 7).

The woman was surprised at his request. After all, he was a Jew, and the Jews had little to do with the Samaritans. And he was a man, and a man would rarely talk with a woman publicly.

In this dialogue Jesus overcame several barriers. The discussion with Nicodemus was with an orthodox Jewish male. This discussion was with a Samaritan, considered totally unorthodox and, at best, a half-caste person who was also female. The racial barrier was crossed, since the Jews had no dealings with the Samaritans. The sexual barrier was overcome, as men did not usually talk with women in public. And the religious barrier fell as a Jew spoke with a Samaritan whose religion was considered suspect and incomplete by the Jews. The gospel regularly crosses the barriers people have erected between people.

Answering her surprised query, Jesus indicated that if she only knew to whom she spoke that he would give her living water. "Living water" (v. 10) usually refers to fresh, flowing water as contrasted with more stagnant water from a well. As often happened, she first understood his statement on a literal, physical level when Jesus actually had a deeper, spiritual meaning in mind. The living water of which he spoke was the life-giving water that would give eternal life.

But she wanted to know how he could draw that water from the well; the well was deep, and he had neither rope nor container with which to draw it from the well. Besides, did he consider himself greater than Jacob who had provided the well?

Jesus answered her question at the literal level first then quickly moved to the spiritual meaning. Everyone who drank from that well would quench physical thirst for only a short time. Water would have to be drawn and drunk again and again. But he could offer her the living water that would be of such satisfaction that one would never have to drink again. It would be as an artesian well of eternal life that sprang up from within the person, giving full and complete satisfaction (v. 14).

Perhaps, remembering her embarrassing visits to the well, that appealed to her. So she asked him for that water so that she would never thirst again and never have to return to the well for water.

Then Jesus asked her to call her husband (v. 16). Why did Jesus ask her to call her husband into the discussion? He was having a satisfactory conversation with the woman herself. Jesus probably asked her to call her husband for two reasons: propriety and strategy. It was proper to call the husband because it was not considered good etiquette for a woman to talk with a man unless her husband was present. It was a strategic move in that it caused her to admit her need. She would have been reluctant to bring her irregular life into the open with a complete stranger. When she answered that she had no husband (v. 17), Jesus revealed that he knew that. She had lived with five husbands and was then living with a man to whom she was not married (v. 18). Although some have found other explanations, it is better to understand it as simply an admission of her guilt.

Seeking to divert the discussion from its uncomfortable, personal direction, the woman asked a religious question. Perceiving that Jesus must have been a prophet, she dragged up the old question between the Jews and the Samaritans about the proper place to worship God (vv. 19-20). The Jews had centered worship in the Temple at Jerusalem; the Samaritans persisted in worshiping at Mount Gerizim even after their temple was destroyed.

But Jesus would not be steered off course. In his answer he freed worship forever from the limitations of place. The "hour" again refers to the time when he would redeem the world through his death on the cross and resurrection from the dead. That time had even then broken into human history through him. The Jews worshiped the God who had revealed himself already as the universal God. Salvation would come from the Jews (v. 22) because they were the prepared people from whom the Messiah would come who would deliver all the world. The Messiah would be a Jew.

Those who truly worship God worship him in spirit and in truth (v. 24). God is spirit and is therefore not confined to any particular place of worship. When one confronts God in complete sincerity (spirit) and in absolute reality (truth) that person can worship God. In the new age of God's redemption through Christ (the Messiah), worship is not restricted by place, sex, or religion but is determined by God himself who is spirit. The reality of God, the truth which

God makes known to persons, is known in Jesus Christ who is God in person.

Still attempting to avoid the direct personal issue that Jesus introduced, the woman admitted her knowledge that at some time, at some place, in some way the Messiah would come and clear up those mysteries (v. 25). Jesus continually refused to be diverted by her tactics and revealed himself as the Messiah (v. 26). He could make this direct reference to his identity in Samaria though he could not have done so in either Judea or Galilee due to the messianic expectations in vogue there. This was his most direct self-assertion of messiahship. It constituted a challenge to respond.

About this time the disciples returned from the city with their lunch. Surprised to find Jesus talking publicly with a woman, none of them questioned his breach of etiquette. They did not question either his conduct or the woman's motive. Apparently, they had become accustomed to his complete freedom of action (v. 27).

But, possibly because of the surprised look on the disciples' faces or possibly because of the burden of her discovery, the woman left quickly. In leaving the well she also left her waterpot. With the burden of the message she had to deliver she did not need to be encumbered with the physical burden of the waterpot. The one who received ministry became a missionary.

Her witness was simple (v. 29). She challenged them to come see a man who had told her everything she had ever done. But her witness was also tentative. The question could actually be rendered, "This man couldn't really be the Christ, could he?" It was as though she expected a negative answer but hoped for a positive answer. When one gives witness to Christ one does not have to be elaborate, dogmatic, or able to answer all the questions. The witness can be simple, direct, and personal. The men of Sychar would hardly have expected theological pronouncements from that woman, anyhow. But they did leave the city to see Jesus.

The disciples, in the meantime, were concerned about Jesus' physical condition. They had left him at the well tired and hungry. Then when they returned he would not eat the food they had brought to him. They urged him to eat (v. 31). But he replied that he had food to eat of which they were not aware. Like the woman, they interpreted his statement literally and even wondered if someone had brought him some food unknown to them (v. 34). But then Jesus expanded his statement to let them know that he got his sustenance and strength from doing the will of God who had sent him to the earth. He received his satisfaction from doing the work of the Father.

The next reflective statement of Jesus to them may have indicated the time of the year: harvest was yet four months away. Or it could have been a current proverbial saying: harvest was four months away so one would not need to rush his activities. Perhaps Jesus then saw the people coming from Sychar to the well and drew the attention of the disciples to them when he urged them to look at the fields that were already ripe for harvest (v. 35). The human harvest represented by the people of Sychar may have already been on its way. The person who reaps a human harvest receives his wages of personal joy and the completed work of the Father who had sent him. In addition to that, those persons whose lives he has touched receive the "fruit" of eternal life. What a significant harvest that is (v. 36): the sower and reaper rejoice together. Anyone who participates in the ultimate harvest is blessed.

Then Jesus used another proverbial saying when he said that one sows and another reaps. In the spiritual harvest of human lives both the sower and the reaper share in the benefits. Many who will reap, reap the benefits of what others have sowed. Others have done the work of sowing and cultivating; that person just showed up for the reaping. But the end result is due to the work of all of them. His immediate reference may have been to the disciples entering into the harvest begun by the preparation of the prophets and John the Baptist's ministry or the work of Jesus himself. The ultimate meaning is that many persons contribute together to the spiritual harvest in human lives (v. 38).

By then the harvest had arrived. The people from Sychar showed up in great number in response to the simple personal testimony of the Samaritan woman (v. 39). At their request for a longer visit, Jesus stayed there for two days. Then many people believed on him because of their personal experience with him (v. 41). They indicated to the woman that they had first been attracted to Jesus by her testimony but then had come to the personal understanding that he was the Savior of the world (v. 42). Faith comes with the witness of others and with personal knowledge and experience with Jesus. In

Jesus there is a new inclusiveness. The relationship of the Jews to the Samaritans demonstrated exclusiveness. And women were also excluded. But the actions of Jesus proved inclusiveness. The Savior of the world included all people in new life who would respond to him in faith.

Healing the Official's Son: A New Life (4:43-54)

After two days in Sychar Jesus resumed his journey to Galilee. Jesus observed that a prophet was not honored in his own country (v. 44), a statement also recorded by the other Gospels (Matt. 13:57; Mark 6:4; Luke 4:24). Did he mean by "his own country" the Judea which he was leaving in which he had been born or the Galilee to which he was headed where he had been reared? It is not clear, but it could apply to each. He was opposed in Jerusalem of Judea and rejected in Nazareth of Galilee. The people of Galilee were anxious to receive him, for some of them had been to the feast in Jerusalem also and had seen the things he had done there.

In Cana of Galilee, the site of his first miracle (2:1-11), the opportunity was given for him to repeat some of those mighty works. An official, likely with Herod's court, living at Capernaum came from the seaside city of Capernaum to the hillside city of Cana to ask Jesus to come heal his son who was at the very point of death (v. 47). Jesus' reply to him seems rather harsh at first. Directed to the people around them as well as to the official, Jesus charged that they would not believe unless they saw signs and wonders (v. 48). After all, that is what they had wanted repeated in their area (v. 45). But the man persisted, asking Jesus to come with him to Capernaum before the child died (v. 49).

Steadfastly refusing to resort to the sensational and spectacular, Jesus simply told the man to go back home, for his son would live. This put the man on the horns of a dilemma. If he refused to go home without Jesus it would indicate that he did not believe his word. If he took Jesus at his word he would return with no visible proof of his son's healing. The man responded by the way of faith. With no visible proof that what Jesus had said was true, with no visible proof that his boy was healed, the official believed Jesus (v. 50). He took Jesus at his word by faith.

The next day as he returned home he was met by his servants

with the welcome news that his son's fever was gone and that he was healing. The official inquired as to the time this took place. When they told him that the fever was gone at the seventh hour (1:00 PM), he knew this was exactly the time that Jesus had told him his son was healed. Without visible proof of the healing, the healing had occurred. It was more than a coincidence; it was the power of God through Jesus Christ giving new life. The official believed on Jesus in the sense of entrusting his life to Jesus. By faith he accepted Jesus as Lord. Those of his household also believed on Jesus in the same way (v. 54). The writer of the gospel recorded that this was the second sign included in the gospel. The first sign had also occurred in Cana.

Three times in this incident the word "live" was used (vv. 50,51,53). Quite obviously, the incident showed that new life was both present and possible through Jesus Christ. As the signs in John's gospel point beyond the event to a truth about God made known in Jesus Christ, this one points to new life through Christ. Jesus Christ gives new life.

In the three events recorded in chapters 3 and 4, Jesus met with a Jew, a Samaritan, and possibly a Gentile. If this official in Herod's court were a Gentile, which is highly probable, then these three persons represent the world Jesus came to save, composed of the Jews, Samaritans, and Gentiles. New life through Jesus Christ is for all people.

Six events have now been presented in the Fourth Gospel. Each of them indicates something of the revelation of Jesus to the world that he had come to save. God and his power to bless was made known through Jesus Christ. Persons must respond in belief.

Reaction (5:1 to 10:42)

With this section the increasing reaction of the Jewish leaders to Jesus is emphasized. That each of the incidents of controversy is set within the context of a Jewish religious festival serves to heighten the dramatic effect of their opposition to Jesus. Jesus had been revealed to the world as God's promised one. The reaction to that revelation was not always positive. Each of these events told something more about the Christ.

Healing a Lame Man: The Authority for Life (5:1-47)

At an unspecified time Jesus went south again to Jerusalem to an unidentified feast. While there he went to a pool by the sheep gate that was surrounded by five porches. Probably it was a double pool with porches all around it and one running between the two pools, thus making five porches. The name of the pool appears variously as Bethzatha (RSV), Bethesda (which means "house of mercy," KJV), or Bethsaida. There is also some difficulty in whether it is a sheep gate, sheep pool, or sheep market that is intended. At any rate, the pool was surrounded by sick and crippled people who were lying under the shade of the porches waiting for an opportuniy to get into the pool. They believed that the pool had healing properties. Specifically, they believed that the first person to enter the pool after the disturbing or bubbling of the waters would be healed. In some versions of the Gospel verses 3*b*-4 give an explanation of the healing properties of the pool being due to an angel stirring the waters periodically. That reference is not found in the oldest manuscripts. But it might explain the presence of the people there.

Jesus found a man there who had been ill for thirty-eight years (v. 5). While it is not indicated how Jesus knew the length of the man's illness, it is clear that Jesus took the initiative in approaching him. When Jesus asked him if he desired to be healed the man replied with a whining excuse. He did not have anyone there who could put him in the pool when the water was stirred. Apparently, he was not willing to take personal responsibility either for his disability or his healing.

But Jesus acted decisively on his behalf. To the man he gave a command to do what he could not do—to rise, to take up his bed, to make no provision for relapse, and to walk—to continue in strength. And he did! He must have neither questioned Jesus nor balked at his command. Immediately the man was healed and walked away with his pallet. He was given no visible proof beforehand that Jesus would heal him. He did not even know who Jesus was (v. 13). He was not asked for a demonstration of his own faith before Jesus acted. In obedience to the command of Jesus the man acted. And he was healed. The water could not heal him, but Jesus could.

This happened on a sabbath (v. 9). So even though the paralytic was healed, a controversy was precipitated. This is the first open hostility to Jesus recorded in John's Gospel. The cause was his attitude toward the sabbath. For the man to carry his bed on the sabbath was a violation of one of the interpretations of the Fourth Commandment. The Jewish leaders accosted the man on the basis of his unlawfully carrying his bed (v. 10) on the sabbath. Unwilling to accept responsibility for that either, he shifted the blame to Jesus who had healed him. But when they questioned him about the identity of the one who had healed him he could not tell them (v. 13). This helpless, hopeless man had not even secured the name of the one who had so blessed him. And Jesus had quietly slipped away from the place which had doubtlessly become crowded when the healing was made known.

As it was Jesus who took the initiative in the man's healing so it was Jesus who took the initiative in finding the man (v. 14). At some unspecified time later Jesus found him in the Temple area. Even though Jesus had not received from the man any admission of guilt or statement of repentance prior to the healing, he warned him that since he was healed he should show his gratitude to God by not sinning. To be a spiritual cripple would be a worse fate than being a physical cripple. The man showed his regard for Jesus by reporting to the Jewish leaders that Jesus was the one who had healed him (v. 15).

This report caused the hostility toward Jesus to surface publicly. The Jewish leaders were more concerned with the offense of healing on the sabbath and carrying the bed than they were with the man's healing. Jesus' reply to them was that God, his Father, worked still on the sabbath in his providential care. He was simply carrying out the work of his Father whose work he had been sent to earth to do (v. 17). This really caused trouble. For one thing, Jesus' view of God ran counter to their view of God. They thought of God as a God of legalism who was more interested in people keeping the interpretations of the commandments. Jesus saw God as a God of compassion who was more concerned with the continual healing of human hurt. Not only had Jesus healed on the sabbath, but he had also claimed equality with God. When Jesus based his defense on intimate relationship with God they correctly interpreted it as a claim of equality with God. This really upset them. And the persecution became public; they sought even to kill him (v. 18).

Even with intimate relationship with the Father, Jesus did not act independently (v. 19). All that he did was what the Father also was doing. He acted in dependent obedience to the Father. The Father loved the Son to the extent that he entrusted to the Son both his will and his works. And greater works would follow. God was up to something greater than the healing of one man. What God would ultimately do in the Son would surely cause them to wonder (v. 20).

One thing that God would do through the Son involved the giving of life (v. 21). The Father could resurrect the dead and give life to them. Jesus indicated that he could also bring the dead to life (physically, as with Lazarus in ch. 11) and could bestow life (spiritually, as with the hopeless man just healed). Life comes through Jesus Christ.

Judgment was another thing that the Father would do through the Son (v. 22). The basis of judgment is the relationship of that person to the Son, Jesus Christ. To fail to receive and follow the Son is to dishonor and reject the Father who sent him. To receive the Christ and to believe on him is to have eternal life, that life of eternal quality that never ends (v. 24). Life comes through Jesus Christ, and the judgment as to whether one has entered into that life is based on whether one has believed the Christ.

The age to come has broken into the present age in Jesus Christ (v. 25). The "hour" or the time when even the dead will hear the voice of God and have life is the present time through Jesus Christ. Both literally and metaphorically, both physically and spiritually, Jesus Christ gives life. It is acting on the authority of God that the Son grants life to those who believe on him. The "Son of man" (v. 27) is a messianic term which indicates that Jesus is both the source of life and the basis of judgment for life. In the time of general resurrection all shall hear this same voice in judgment, and destiny will be determined by the life based on decision about the Christ (v. 29). Jesus had accepted the two prerogatives of God in the exercising of judgment and the giving of life. Both the life of regeneration and the life of resurrection came through Jesus Christ.

Where did Jesus get his authority? Jesus did not rest his actions upon his own authority but upon his doing the will of the one who sent him (v. 30). He did not have the traditional authority of either the family tradition of the priests or the extended training of the rabbis. And he had even violated the Law in healing on the sabbath. Nor would he depend upon self-assertion, as did many messianic pretenders. He would not give witness to himself (v. 31); testimony could not rest on a single witness but had to be confirmed by others. Jesus piled witness upon witness to attest to his authority.

The first witness he called was God himself, the Father. First alluding to God in verse 30 as the one who sent him and in verse 32 as the one whose testimony is true, he pointed to the Father as a witness in verses 37-38. God, the Father, was the one who had sent him. They had heard the voice of God before, but they had not physically seen God. But they did not have the word of God living in them because they had not believed on Christ, the one sent by God. This is a reflection of the judgment mentioned in verse 24.

A second witness was John the Baptist (vv. 32-34). John had borne witness to Jesus. They had gone out to see him as a light that burned in the darkness. But, even though they rejoiced for a while in that light, they did not follow that light to the Christ.

The works of Jesus himself were a third witness to him (v. 36). These works were done through the power of the Father and as an expression of the will of the Father who had sent him. But that the works of Christ were not self-authenticating is seen in their response to the healing of the paralytic man earlier in this chapter. They had seen that the man was healed by Jesus; yet they still did not believe.

The Scriptures themselves stood as a fourth witness to Jesus (vv. 39-44). Obviously, the Old Testament Scriptures were meant. They would search the Scriptures to find mention of the Messiah. Those very Scriptures pointed to him, but the people did not believe them. His glory or honor did not come from people, anyway; it came from God. And it was obvious that the love of God was not in them or they would have received Jesus. Jesus had come in the name—by the power and authority—of the Father. They had not followed him while they had chased after other messianic pretenders at other times. Glory had come from God, and they had not recognized it.

A fifth witness to Jesus and thus accusation against them came from Moses (vv. 45-47). Since Moses was considered both the greatest prophet and the author of the Pentateuch, his witness to Jesus would parallel the witness of Scripture to him. But they did not follow that witness to Jesus either. It would be too much to think that they would believe the words of Jesus when they would not believe the writings of Moses.

From this discourse it becomes apparent that the Jewish leaders did not accept Jesus as the Son of God sent into the world to do the work of God. And from this discourse it becomes apparent that is exactly how Jesus saw himself. They saw him only as one who broke the law and assumed an equality with God. For that they could not let him live. Jesus asserted an authority for life that was based on his divine mission from God the Father.

Feeding the Five Thousand: The Bread of Life (6:1-71)

Another unspecified time sequence places Jesus back in Galilee. This has led some to think that chapter 6 should precede chapter 5. However, this indefiniteness along with the lack of identification of the particular mountain or hill where Jesus went with his disciples (v. 3) only serves to indicate that the writer of the Fourth Gospel was more interested in theological truth than he was in either chronological or geographical precision. The "other side" of the Sea of Galilee refers to the east shore of the lake as opposed to the west shore around Capernaum (v. 1). Notice, too, that the lake was given two identifications. The Sea of Galilee was the name by which it was known in the area and would be recognized by Jewish readers. Tiberius was a city on the western shore of the Sea of Galilee, built in AD 20 by Herod and named after the Emperor. Likely, the lake was known by that name later and would be recognized as such by other readers.

At a time close to the Passover season Jesus went with his disciples to the eastern shore of the Sea of Galilee to a mountain which was possibly a place to which they regularly went for rest and teaching. Assuming the position of a rabbi or teacher, Jesus sat and taught his disciples. The reference to the time of the Passover could be more than incidental considering what happened later. The Passover was a time when the Jews considered the deliverance and care God gave to the people of Israel during the Exodus experience, including his feeding them with manna, bread from heaven.

By this time great crowds of people were following Jesus. But their reason for following him was more physical than spiritual. They were interested in the healing that he kept on giving to folks who hurt (v. 2). This great crowd of people was impressed with the healing they had seen and found Jesus and his disciples at the mountain.

As Jesus was teaching he noticed the approach of the multitude. So he asked Philip, who was from Bethsaida and thus a native of the area, where they could secure enough food to feed all those folks (v. 4). The question was designed to test Philip and his faith, for Jesus already knew what he would do (v. 6). In despair Philip answered that two hundred denarii would not be enough to buy a little for each of them to eat, to say nothing of filling them. A denarius was the usual daily wage of a working person. As far as Philip was concerned, the situation was hopeless.

Andrew, identified as Simon Peter's brother, had also been on the lookout. He had located one little boy with a lunch. But speaking with almost the same kind of hopelessness, he asked what that would do among so many people (v. 9). The five barley loaves were small, flat, round loaves eaten by poor people. The two fish were small pickled fish used to make the bread more palatable. The little boy had his lunch with him; but the lunch was a poor person's lunch of five small cracker-like loaves and two small relish-like fish. That apparently was all the food Andrew had been able to locate, and he doubted that anything could be done with it. That, too, made the situation hopeless.

At a time of human hopelessness Jesus took over. He had them seat the people in an orderly fashion on the grassy area. The count reached about five thousand men, without any indication of the number of women and children (v. 10). At a time when human knowledge, ingenuity, and resourcefulness failed, Jesus acted.

In the only miracle recorded by all four Gospels, Jesus took the bread that had been given to him by the boy, blessed it, and gave it to the people. He did the same with the fish. And it was enough to satisfy the hunger of everyone there (v. 11). What had seemed to be a hopeless situation had been turned into a scene of hope by the power of God working through the Christ. A little bit given into the hands of Jesus became a lot.

Not only was Jesus able to meet their need, he supplied more than enough. After everyone had eaten to capacity, Jesus had the disciples gather up what was left over. The resources of God's grace are to be neither squandered nor wasted. Twelve baskets full of the leftovers were collected (v. 13). There were twelve disciples; each of them were able to fill a basket with the leftovers. There were also twelve tribes in Israel. At a time when the people were thinking of how God had provided bread for Israel during the wilderness wanderings they were shown that God through Jesus Christ provided more than was adequate for human needs. What Jesus gives is more than a sufficiency.

And the people recognized that. They began to express the belief that Jesus might indeed be the prophet greater than Moses whom the Scripture prophesied would come into the world (Deut. 18:15). Messianic expectations were high in Galilee. Moses had provided them with manna in the wilderness; this prophet could do even better (v. 14).

Sensing that the people were about to launch a movement to make him king, Jesus slipped off into the hilly area by himself (v. 15). For the people this would be the perfect kind of king: he could heal physical hurts, and he could relieve physical hunger. But this was not the kind of Messiah Jesus would be. He had already decided that in his wilderness temptation experience. He would, instead, deliver human hearts, giving forgiveness and new life. His would be a spiritual kingdom of God's rule in human lives that transcended time and place rather than a political kingdom limited to one time and place.

By the time of evening the disciples went to their boat to start their trip back across the Sea of Galilee. Jesus had slipped off alone and had not rejoined the disciples at this time even though they probably expected him (v. 17). Wanting to get back before too late in the evening, the disciples started across the lake without him. But, as could easily happen on a landlocked mountain-ringed lake, the wind changed and the Sea of Galilee became an angry, wave-frothed sea (v. 18). From the notation that they had already rowed three or four miles it would seem that they were probably halfway across the lake when the storm arose and the water got dangerous. Suddenly, across the wind-whipped, churning waves the disciples saw someone coming to them across the water. Not recognizing Jesus, and likely thinking it was an apparition of some sort, they were afraid. They had probably already begun to fear for their lives in the storm.

In their fear and consternation they heard a familiar voice saying, "It is I; do not be afraid" (v. 20). In another situation of human hopelessness and fear Jesus had given hope and reassurance. Taking Jesus aboard ship they were immediately at their destination on the western shore, probably Capernaum. The fourth and fifth signs in

John's Gospel occur in quick succession. They each teach that in those times of human hopelessness and helplessness deliverance and strength come from Jesus Christ. The reassuring voice of Jesus as it speaks to humans in times of helpless fear gives hope and help.

Possibly hoping to catch Jesus when he came down the mountain, many of the crowd had not left the place where Jesus had fed the five thousand men. Realizing that there had only been one boat there and that Jesus had not boarded that boat with the disciples, they could not understand where he had gone. When other boats came into the area from Tiberius—probably fishing boats at work on the lake—the people boarded those boats as they realized that neither Jesus nor his disciples were still there. Crossing the Sea of Galilee to Capernaum they still tried to find Jesus.

When they found Jesus they only asked him one question: how did he get there? (v. 25). Apparently the miracle of walking on the water was known only to his disciples. The people whom he had earlier fed were unaware of how he had crossed the lake.

Jesus answered a totally superficial question with a spiritual truth. They had already forgotten the sign involved in their feeding. Their only reason for looking for him was to be fed again. Jesus then warned them not to spend all their time working for those things that perished, but to look for the enduring, unperishing food that the Son of man could provide for them. God had given his seal of approval to that one (v. 27). Like the pattern also used in John's Gospel, Jesus followed a sign or an event with a discourse. He pointed them to the source of the satisfying spiritual sufficiency.

But they were so literal and material in their understanding of what Jesus said that they missed his reference to the imperishable food of God's grace and picked up instead on his reference to labor. They wanted to know what kind of work they would have to do in order to do the works of God (v. 28). Religion that rests on grace rather than works is always difficult to understand or to accept.

So Jesus informed them that what God desired was for them to believe on the One whom he had sent. He had earlier (v. 27) made a reference to the Son of man, which was a messianic title. The work that pleases God is belief in what he has done, not a works kind of righteousness that tries to earn God's favor.

Understanding the reference to himself as the Son of man, they then wanted to know what kind of sign he would give to prove to them that he was the Son of man. Did he have a particular work that he could do that would convince them (v. 30)? Moses had shown them a spectacular sign. He had fed them manna, bread from heaven, while on the wilderness wandering. While it is not an exact quotation, verse 31 likely refers to Psalm 78:24-25. If, as some suspected (v. 14), he were the prophet greater than Moses that God had sent to deliver them then he would have to produce a work greater than Moses before they would believe. How soon they had forgotten what he had done just the day before in feeding the five thousand men! What greater sign could they want?

Jesus corrected their statement at two points. In the first place, it was not Moses that had given them the bread from heaven. God had given the bread from heaven. And Jesus identified God as his father (v. 32). In calling the one who gave the true bread from heaven his father, Jesus was identifying himself with God.

And the second point at which he corrected them was that the gift of God which is the true bread of heaven was not a one-time gift. It was a gift of God that continued to come from heaven to humans and to give life. The life-giving gift of God was continuous. Even though he did not draw out the implication clearly at this point, the implication is that the gift of God's true Bread of life is found in him who had already identified himself with God.

Showing their literal, materialistic orientation, the people asked that they might have this real bread of life (v. 34). Echoing the request of the woman at the well who asked for the living water so that she would not have to draw from the well again (4:15), they asked for the Bread of life so they would not hunger again.

Then Jesus clarified his statement when he made the first of seven claims found in the Gospel of John (6:35; 8:12; 10:7,11; 11:25; 14:6; 15:1). Each of the claims is introduced with the emphatic declaration, "I am." And each of the claims represents a particular relationship of Jesus to the spiritual needs of humankind. Here he claimed, "I am the bread of life" (v. 35). He was that which gives spiritual sustenance and strength to an individual. Earlier he had referred to the bread from heaven (v. 32) and the Bread of life (v. 33), but at this point he claimed to be the Bread of life. It is through Jesus himself and belief on him that a person finds life and spiritual sustenance.

They had seen him, but they had not believed on him. He had

come down from heaven to do the will of the Father. They would do God's will, the will of the Father, when they believed on him. All of those who believed on him he would not lose; each one would be saved to the end. And at the end, every one who had eternal life through belief on Jesus would be raised up (v. 40).

There is an interesting play in this passage on Jesus "coming down" from heaven and persons "coming to" him in belief. Seven times in these verses Jesus indicated that he had come down from heaven (vv. 33,38,41,42,50,51,58). For a person to know the salvation and spiritual sustenance that the Father provides, that person has to come to Jesus in belief. Jesus is both the gift and the giver. And the gift is received only by coming to the giver.

Jesus' statement that he was the Bread of life who had come down from heaven caused murmuring among the Jewish people reminiscent of their murmuring against Moses in the wilderness. Usually "the Jews" refers to the Judean Jewish leaders who opposed Jesus. In this case, it refers to Galilean Jews. So the term can be an inclusive term to include all those Jewish leaders who opposed Jesus. That they were from Galilee is obvious when they interpreted his statement literally again. They thought it preposterous that he could claim to come from heaven when they knew his earthly parents in the Galilean village of Nazareth (v. 42).

Ignoring their literal interpretation by telling them not to murmur or complain among themselves, Jesus emphasized the divine initiative in salvation (v. 44). No one could come to the Father in belief unless that one were drawn by the Father. And every one who responds to that divine initiative by coming to the Son will receive salvation. None will be lost. Quoting Isaiah 54:13, Jesus indicated that all would be taught by the Father. The one who really hears the teachings of God will respond to his Son, Jesus.

Repeating the thought found in the Prologue (1:18), Jesus reminded them that no one had seen the Father but the Son. That one who had come from the Father was the only one who had seen the Father. By belief in him persons could have eternal life. Then again Jesus made his claim: "I am the bread of life" (v. 48). It is he who has come from the Father, and it is he who brings eternal life from the Father. Jesus identified himself with God.

Earlier (vv. 30-31) the Jewish people had demanded from Jesus a sign greater than the sign of Moses, whom they credited with the manna from heaven, before they would believe. Jesus then showed them how the bread of life that he had was different from the manna during the wilderness. As the Bread of life Jesus gives life. Those who ate the manna died. But the person who partakes of the Bread of life will not die: that person has eternal life. Jesus claimed that he was this living bread (v. 51) which promised eternal life. And he even drew it out more clearly when he said that the bread which he gave was his own flesh (v. 51).

Knowing the end of the story of the crucifixion and resurrection of Jesus Christ, it is quite obvious that his reference is to his death. In giving himself, his flesh, for us on the cross he made possible the eternal life that is available to all who come to him in belief. Those who come are those drawn to him by the Father through the Holy Spirit.

Again, as in verse 41, the Jewish people murmured at his statement. Taking the statement of eating his flesh with gross literalism they were highly offended at what sounded like cannibalism to them. A typical teaching technique in John's Gospel was for Jesus to make an ambiguous statement, to which the people would give an objection, and then for Jesus to show what he really meant by his reply to their objection. How could a person give his flesh to eat? they asked (v. 52).

For the fourth time in this discussion (see also vv. 26,32,47) Jesus used the solemn words, "Truly, truly, I say to you" (v. 53), which indicated a serious statement that must be heeded. Using another teaching technique of the Fourth Gospel, he first stated negatively (v. 54) then positively (v. 55) that anyone who has life in Christ must not only eat his flesh but also drink his blood. This was a graphic way of saying that a person must take Christ into his innermost being; he must put Christ within himself. This is the person who abides in Christ and in whom Christ abides. Abiding in Christ is an important concept. Belief in Jesus is not temporary and fleeting; it calls for a faith for the long haul, for abiding in that belief and thus in Christ. Jesus was sent by the living Father and has life because of the Father (v. 57). And the person who has eternal life lives because of Jesus Christ. Christ has become a part of that life. The contrast is once again drawn between those who ate of the manna in the wilderness and died just as anyone else and those who partake of Christ and have eternal life.

These words were spoken in the synagogue in Nazareth (v. 59). While it is not stated, the impression is gained that the conversation started outside as the people found Jesus in Capernaum (v. 25). If that is true, the discussion may have started by the seashore and moved into the synagogue. Or it may have all taken place in the synagogue. But where the scene was set was not as important to the writer of the Gospel as the fact that in the synagogue, where the Law of Moses was regularly read, Jesus had spoken truths that indicated he was superior to the Law. He had contrasted the sustenance which God had provided through their leader Moses with the life that he would provide. He had said that one must eat his flesh and drink his blood, which was contrary to the Law. He had identified himself with the Father. He had made it clear that the only way one would have a saving eternal relationship with the Father was through belief in him. He had split absolutely with the synagogue.

This caused some murmuring among the disciples (v. 60). The previous murmuring or complaining at what he had said came from those who opposed him. This was from some who followed him. The word *disciple* means a learner. These are people who were attracted to him and followed after him. They must be distinguished from the twelve whom we also usually label as the disciples.

The basis of their murmuring was that what Jesus had just said was a hard statement. By that they did not mean that it was hard to understand but that it was hard to follow and accept.

Many have wondered if this section has to do with the Lord's Supper. In fact, many people interpret it as applying directly to the Lord's Supper. This is not likely the proper meaning of the passage. For one thing, it would require a reading back into the discussion an event that occurred later for it to have any reference to the Lord's Supper. Also, this discussion indicates that life, eternal life, comes through eating the flesh and drinking the blood of Jesus. That comes through accepting Christ into one's life, not by the observance of the Lord's Supper. While the passage may not refer directly to the Lord's Supper, it is true that it helps in the understanding of the Lord's Supper by pointing up that one does not partake of the life of God without a personal acceptance of the sacrifice of Jesus. The Christian's entire life and worship is dependent upon Jesus. John's Gospel does not record the act of instituting the Lord's Supper.

Jesus knew that they were complaining about what he had said (v. 61). So he said to them that, if they had trouble accepting that statement, they would surely have trouble accepting him ascending to heaven from which he had come. The Spirit of God gives life. The words that he had spoken had both Spirit and life in them. By accepting them persons could have life through the Spirit of God.

Jesus knew that some of them would not believe him or his words. He knew from the beginning that some would not believe him and that one would betray him (v. 64). That is the very reason that he had asserted that no one could come to faith in him without the divine initiative, unless the Father had drawn that one to belief in Christ (v. 65).

This led to a division of the people. Those who had followed Jesus simply out of attraction to him or curiosity about him departed from him (v. 66). First there was opposition; now there was desertion. It became apparent that Jesus was no common teacher; he had claimed an identification with God and demanded an acceptance of himself. Those who were not prepared to make that kind of complete commitment turned away from him.

Seeing this rejection, Jesus then turned to the twelve and tested their loyalty. He asked if they would go away also (v. 67). It is no surprise that Simon Peter answered for the apostolic group of twelve loyal followers. No. They would not depart from him. They would not leave, for he alone had the words that would bring life to persons. There was no one else to whom they could go for life-giving words. And the second reason was that they had come to believe that Jesus was "the Holy One of God" (vv. 68-69). That was not a common term to be used for Jesus. By the use of that messianic term Simon Peter was identifying Jesus with God. He was placing Jesus with God and not with humankind. This confession voiced by Simon Peter for the twelve followers of Jesus is the closest that John's Gospel has to the great confession at Caesarea Philippi recorded in the Synoptic Gospels. It is John's form of that confession. They had decided to follow Jesus.

But Jesus would not be swept away by that confession. He had already seen the number of people who followed him dwindle from five thousand men to twelve disciples, one of whom would betray him. Jesus responded to the confession by saying that he had chosen those twelve (v. 70), but even one of them would be unfaithful. He had continually emphasized that those who would come to belief in him would be chosen by God.

What did he mean by calling Judas Iscariot "a devil?" (v. 71). Jesus did not mean that Judas was the devil himself. Neither did he mean that Judas would not be responsible for his act of betraying Jesus because the devil made him do it. Jesus meant, instead, that Judas Iscariot was doing the work of the devil; he was following the devil's purposes.

Going to the Feast of the Tabernacles: The Water of Life (7:1-52)

In another indefinite time frame the observation is made that Jesus continued a ministry in Galilee rather than in Judea. The reason was that the Jewish leaders in Judea had already threatened his life (5:18).

The time arrived for the annual observance of the Feast of the Tabernacles. The Feast of the Tabernacles was observed in the fall with the dual purpose of celebration and thanksgiving for the fall harvest, especially the grape harvest, and commemoration of the wilderness wanderings. One of the three feasts which Jewish men were required to attend, it got its name from the use of temporary booths or tabernacles erected in the vineyards during the harvest to guard the fields. These would also remind the people of the movable tents in which they lived during the wandering in the wilderness. Lasting a full week, eight days including a sabbath added at the end, it was a favorite festival of the people.

When the time came for the people to leave Galilee for the pilgrimage to Jerusalem the brothers of Jesus urged him to go to Jerusalem to publicly proclaim his mission (v. 3). The identity of the brothers has created a question. Were they half-brothers of Jesus, sons of Mary and Joseph? Or were they sons of Joseph by a previous marriage? Or were they simply cousins of Jesus? There is no biblical reason to think that they were not half-brothers, sons of Mary and Joseph, with Jesus being the eldest. These brothers were unbelievers (v. 5). Joseph was not Jesus' actual father, as Jesus was the Son of God.

Their suggestion should be understood more as a challenge than counsel. Jesus was being challenged to go to the central site of Jewish faith and life to manifest himself rather than in the peripheral area of Galilee. There the people who had been attracted to him initially could follow him. If he were to have a movement it would have to be publicly proclaimed. Centering it in Galilee was almost like carrying it out secretly.

But Jesus consistently refused to be pushed into action (v. 6). As with the first miracle in Cana (2:1-11), Jesus would not be forced to assert his messiahship. His time had not yet come, the hour when he would be revealed as God's anointed through his death and resurrection. The brothers faced no such danger. The world did not hate them because they were identified with the world. It did hate Jesus because his teachings brought the world under judgment. They could go up to the feast. He was not going up to the feast because his time for manifestation had not yet arrived. The term "going up" often was used to refer to his ascension to the Father. He would go up to the Father when the hour of his manifestation as Messiah would come. This was not the time. So Jesus stayed in Galilee (v. 9).

After his brothers left for Jerusalem and the feast, Jesus finally went also (v. 10). But he did not organize a tour or travel with a group. Quietly, he entered Jerusalem.

The people were expecting him there (v. 11). But there was a division of opinion about him. Some thought that he was a good man doing good things. Others felt that he was leading people astray (v. 12). Because of the fear of hostility from the Jewish leaders, however, these were not open discussions (v. 13).

Halfway through the Feast of Tabernacles Jesus showed up and publicly taught in the Temple precincts. The people, many of whom apparently had not known him previously, were astonished at his teaching. Their questions (v. 15) concerning his teaching without training does not imply illiteracy. It indicates that he taught without rabbinical theological training and certification. The rabbis based their interpretations upon precedent. Jesus was teaching with authority, without appeal to precedent.

This brought up the question of his authority. Jesus rooted his authority in the Father who had sent him (v. 16). His teaching was not of his own invention but in accordance with the will of the Father. Then he gave three lines of support for his teaching. The first had to do with the will of God (v. 17). The person who really wants to do the will of God would see that the teaching of Jesus was consistent with rather than contrary to the revealed will of God. The second support concerned his selfless ministry. It was obvious that what he had done was not for self-glorification (v. 18). A way to judge the authenticity of a messenger is whether the attention is turned to him or to God. Jesus always pointed to the Father. The third argument concerned the place of the Law. They cherished the Law as given by Moses, but they did not keep the Law (v. 19). If they had really been interested in keeping the Law they would not have been trying to kill Jesus.

At this the people protested. How did he know they were trying to kill him? He must have been demon possessed to have this kind of supernatural knowledge (v. 20). This statement must have come from Galilean pilgrims unaware of the plot against his life. Or perhaps this decision had been made by the leaders and the people were not aware of it. At any rate, there was not such opposition to him from the people themselves that they were ready to kill him.

Jesus answered by reminding them that he had done one deed of healing a lame man on the sabbath (5:2-9) and they sought to kill him because of it (v. 21). They had missed the intention of the Law altogether. And he proved his allegation by one illustration.

Circumcision was one element of the Law. Not actually instituted by the Mosaic Law since it went back to the time of Abraham, circumcision was included in the Mosaic Law as a sign of the covenant. Each Jewish male child was circumcised on the eighth day. If a boy baby was born on the sabbath this meant that his circumcision would occur on the sabbath to keep the requirements of the Law. They were inconsistent at this point themselves. They would allow one portion of the body to be treated on the sabbath, but Jesus had made a whole body well on the sabbath (v. 23). They should not make such superficial judgments. Judgments should be consistent and according to the scriptural intentions (v. 24).

What Jesus said made sense. The citizens of Jerusalem were impressed by him and his teachings. But they were also confused. If Jesus was indeed the man the leaders were trying to kill, why was he allowed to continue to teach publicly? Could it be that the authorities knew that he was really the Christ, the Messiah? (v. 26).

Whereas the people had previously questioned the authority of Jesus, they now questioned the origin of Jesus (v. 27). Referring to a popular belief that the Messiah would appear suddenly and unexpectedly, they pointed out in answer to the question of his messiahship that they knew where he had come from. He had come from Nazareth in Galilee. They thought that no one would know either the parents or the place of origin of the Messiah.

In his answer, Jesus indicated that they thought they knew his origin—from Nazareth with Mary and Joseph as his parents—but that they really did not know (v. 28). He was not self-appointed. They could not know that because they did not know the Father in faith. Jesus found his origin in the Father—"I came from him"—and his mission from the Father—"he sent me" (v. 29). He both came from and was sent by the Father.

This brought an attempt to arrest him. But no one took him. The reason that he was not arrested at this time was found in his divine purpose. His "hour" had not yet come. The time in God's purpose when Jesus would be revealed as the Savior through his death and resurrection had not arrived (v. 30). It would come in God's good time.

Many of the people who were there believed on Jesus. They did not think it conceivable that anyone, even the Messiah, could do more signs than Jesus had done. From that line of reasoning, he had to be the deliverer sent by God (v. 31).

Knowing that the people were divided in their assessment of Jesus between devotion, doubt, and derision the Jewish leaders acted against him. In an unusual alliance of the Pharisees and the chief priests who were Sadducees the decision was made to arrest him. But when the arresting officers approached, Jesus spoke to them in a puzzling manner.

Hinting at his coming death, he told them that he would remain there a little longer then he would go to the one who sent him (v. 33). They would look for him, but they would not find him because they could not go where he had gone. As his coming from the Father to the earth implied a descent, so his return to the Father from the earth implied an ascent. Since they had not been where he had been neither could they go where he would go.

The people then wondered where he would go that they could not find him. By now he was a well-known figure even though the popularity of his ministry had peaked with his dramatic portrayal of the cost of discipleship. He could hardly move in a city packed with tourists to a place where they would not find him. So they supposed that perhaps he would slip out of the country and conduct a ministry among the Greek-speaking Jews of the Dispersion. Those Jews who lived outside the country of Palestine, as some had since the Babylonian Exile, were known as the Dispersion. They were dispersed from their homeland (v. 35). They discussed among themselves what he meant to the extent that they failed to arrest him. As they had questioned his authority and his origin, so they questioned his destination.

Interestingly enough, by his return to the Father the message and ministry of Jesus was extended ultimately to those dispersed in other places, both Jews and Gentiles.

Jesus had showed up at the Feast of the Tabernacles in midweek. Then on the climactic day, the last day of the Feast—which was probably the seventh day rather than the sabbath day that had been added to it—he made an announcement. Up to this point no record has been given of the teaching of Jesus at the Feast, just the controversies. Then the teaching is given in both a claim and a challenge to commitment (vv. 37-38).

One of the features of the Feast of the Tabernacles was the daily carrying of a jar of water from the pool of Siloam to the Temple. Each morning a procession of priests carried the water, which was poured into a bowl at the altar while the trumpet sounded and the people shouted. This was an expression of thanksgiving for the water in the wilderness wanderings and the rain for the harvest, as well as a prayer for rain for the coming year.

It was against this symbolic background that Jesus stood to proclaim to the people that if anyone thirsted, he should come to him to drink and that one who drank from him would have his spiritual thirst quenched. While it is not absolutely clear whether the scriptural allusion refers to the life-giving water flowing from the heart of the Christ who gives the water from God or from the believer's heart, it probably refers to the Christ. The scriptural quotation is not exact but seems to be an allusion to such passages as Isaiah 43:18-21, 55:1, and 58:11. Jesus himself had promised living water in 4:14. Just as Jesus had earlier used eating his flesh and drinking his blood (6:53-56) to mean to believe on him, so he now used accepting the Water of life that he offered to mean to believe on him.

The writer of the Fourth Gospel then made one of his explanatory remarks (v. 39) that the reference to living water was really a reference to the Holy Spirit. While Jesus was present on earth the Holy Spirit was present with him. When Jesus ascended to the Father the Holy Spirit was poured out on the believers at the Day of Pentecost. Anticipating that experience and explaining it to the readers, the Gospel writer let them know that all who believed on Jesus received the Holy Spirit. This would be evident after his glorification which came with his crucifixion, resurrection, and ascension.

Jesus' statements further confused the crowd of people. Some of them thought that he was the Moses-like prophet predicted in Deuteronomy 18:15 who would precede the Messiah (v. 40). But others were convinced that he must be the Christ, the Greek expression for the Hebrew word *Messiah* (v. 41). This conclusion was countered by the quotation of Micah 5:2 that the Messiah would come from Bethlehem in Judea (v. 42). Speculative theology, proof texting from the Scripture, and preconceived notions caused division, as they normally do. It is ironic that the very same passage that was used to prove the messiahship of Jesus was also used against his messiahship. Since mention is made of his origin several times in this chapter it must have been a subject of conversation among the crowd. Apparently there was a great deal of speculation that he must be the Messiah. Even some of the crowd wanted to arrest him, but the Temple police returned without him (v. 44).

When the Temple police returned to the religious authorities without Jesus in hand they were immediately asked for an explanation (v. 45). Their reply was that "No man ever spoke like this man!" (v. 46). They may have been emphasizing the impact of his content, or the authority with which he spoke, or the observation that no mere man could speak like that, or all three meanings.

The coalition of Sadducees and Pharisees mentioned apparently was the Sanhedrin, a council of seventy elders composed of both groups which the Roman government allowed to rule in religious matters. Sometimes it is simply called the council. Although the Pharisees and Sadducees differed greatly theologically, they were united in their belief that Jesus had to be suppressed.

Their exalted opinion of themselves is evident in their reply to the arresting officers when they asked if they, too, had been so led astray to believe on Jesus (v. 47). Then they capped their argument with the observation that none of their number had believed on Jesus. They knew the Law well. In fact, the Pharisees specialized in keeping the Law. They thought that if people who knew the Law as they did had not turned to Jesus, certainly people as unskilled in the interpretation of the Law as the crowd should not be trusted. They were trapped in tradition. Their authority was themselves. They did not trust the instincts of the people without specialized theological training to recognize valid spiritual truths. But they overlooked the obvious fact that the crowd knew enough to know the supposed place of origin of the Christ.

But there was one of their number who had known Jesus in a closer relationship. Nicodemus, identified as the one who had gone to Jesus previously (3:1-15) and apparently a member of the council, tentatively spoke up (v. 40). His question was phrased as a legal question: the Law gave an accused person the opportunity for his own defense (v. 51). In that charged atmosphere of hatred and bigotry that tentative testimony may have been all that Nicodemus could hope to do. He apparently attempted to steer the conversation back to a legal and rational hearing rather than an emotional and prejudiced conclusion.

They quickly silenced Nicodemus with an accusation (v. 52). In no mood to be either rational or legal they asked Nicodemus if he were a Galilean also. This was both an accusation and an attempt to silence him. They knew who he was and where he was from. Jesus' strongest support had come from Galilee. Was he one of them? Then they challenged him to search the Scripture and see if any prophet had ever come from Galilee. They obviously had overlooked Jonah and were blind to the fact that God could raise up a prophet from anywhere he would. But they were too contemptuous of the Galileans and too opposed to Jesus to bother with that.

Jesus had offered them the water of life. But they had become so tied up in quibbling over the water and questioning its source that they refused to drink it.

Meeting the Woman in Adultery: The Forgiver in Life (7:53 to 8:11)

Following their discussion and the accusation against Nicodemus, the group of religious leaders broke up and went home. Jesus had already gone to the Mount of Olives where he spent the night. This is the only reference in the Fourth Gospel to Jesus spending the evenings at the Mount of Olives, even though the other Gospels mention it. It coincides with other references to his teaching in the Temple in the daytime and spending the evening on the Mount of Olives.

There is practically unanimous agreement that this section was not originally in the Gospel of John at this place. In most of the earlier manuscripts of the New Testament it is not there, and where it is included it shows up at different places. This is reflected in how it is treated in translations of the New Testament. In the Revised Standard Version it is in italics at the bottom of the page. In other translations it is set off by an asterisk or brackets.

In some manuscripts this account follows John 21:24. In others it follows Luke 21:38. Some interpreters feel this material is more like Luke than John. Nevertheless, it finally came to be placed here. It can be treated as authentic history with the understanding that it was probably not a part of this Gospel at this place when the Gospel was first written.

After spending the night on the Mount of Olives Jesus returned to the Temple the next morning to teach. While teaching, the scribes and Pharisees brought a woman to him. Indelicately and insensitively standing her before him in the midst of the crowd, they made a charge against her and demanded a decision from him (vv. 3-4). The charge was that she had been caught in the very act of adultery. Of her guilt there was no doubt. The decision that they demanded of him was whether she should be pronounced guilty and executed by stoning.

This is the only reference in John's Gospel to the scribes. A professional group of writers in a society where everyone was not literate, their specialty was the study of the Law. In copying and writing the Law they had to know the Law. Many of them were Pharisees, but a scribe was not necessarily a Pharisee. In the other Gospels scribes and Pharisees were often seen working in concert, but this is their only mention in the Fourth Gospel.

Actually, in demanding the decision from Jesus they had twisted the Law a bit. In Leviticus 20:10 and Deuteronomy 22:22 the Law is that both the guilty parties should be put to death. In Deuteronomy

22:23 the reference is to a betrothed virgin who had committed adultery being put to death by stoning. So they had really put together some references to claim that the Mosaic Law demanded death by stoning for a guilty adulteress.

What they wanted to do was to put Jesus in a dilemma from which he could not escape. If he said to stone her he would violate the Roman law in pronouncing a death sentence without Roman authority. If he said to free her it would appear that he was soft on sin or ignoring the Mosaic Law.

The whole thing was obviously a trap. If she had been caught in the act of adultery there had to be another party to the act. Where was he? Apparently he had been allowed to escape. Maybe she had even been set up for this purpose. The attitude is that of a lynch mob. They seemed to have no plan for a trial. They were not concerned with justice. They had no sensitivity for the woman. But they did want to trap Jesus. They demanded a decision from him.

Jesus did not answer them but stooped down and began to write in the dust (v. 6). Any answer to what he wrote is speculation. He could have written a portion of the Law, or the names of those before him, or as a Roman judge the sentence he would pronounce, or nothing at all. He may have just doodled in the dust to gain time and to allow them to think about what they were doing.

As they continued to press him for a decision (v. 7), Jesus simply said that the one who was without sin should throw the first rock and continued to draw in the dirt. One by one, as in a procession, they left, starting with the eldest—who would presumably be the leaders. Under those conditions, no one of them was qualified to begin the lynching.

Jesus then looked up to the woman and asked where they were. Were there no accusers? She replied that no one was left to condemn her. And Jesus said that he would not pronounce a sentence on her either (v. 11). It is illustrative of the way that Jesus would "judge no one" (v. 15). Judgment cannot be based on one's own life but on God's revealed will. They had no real basis for condemning her to death.

That Jesus did not condemn her did not mean that he condoned her actions. He challenged her to go from that place and to change her life completely. He was not a man who would exploit her but one who would forgive her. Mercy was a motivation for a changed life.

Discussing at the Feast of the Tabernacles: The Light of the World (8:12-59)

At another unspecified time during the Feast of Tabernacles Jesus made his second great claim when he said, "I am the light of the world" (v. 12). He went on to explain that the person who followed him would not walk in moral and spiritual darkness but would walk in the light of life.

One of the features of the Feast of Tabernacles was the lighting of large golden lampstands in the Court of the Women on the first night of the feast and possibly on other nights. These lights that illuminated the entire courtyard were a reminder of the pillar of fire that accompanied the children of Israel by night during their wilderness wanderings. If these were not lighted each night, and Jesus made a claim at a time when they were not lighted in the courtyard where they would have stood, the claim is even more emphatic. In both the Old and New Testaments light was used as a symbol of God. The true light of God's grace and glory was expressed in Jesus Christ.

Ignoring the claim, the Pharisees jumped to the validity of his witness. It seemed the claim of an egotist since it was uncorroborated by other witnesses (v. 13). Jesus' response to them indicated that they could not ascertain the validity of his witness because they did not understand its context. They knew neither his origin nor his destination. Since they did not know the Father who had sent him they could not understand his witness to himself. His judgment was not according to their standards. Their standard of judgment was external appearances. His standard of judgment rested on the truth of God. While he did not judge anyone by their external standards (v. 15) his very presence was a judgment of persons. Persons were judged in the light of God's truth (v. 16).

Even their own Law to which they gave such credence called for two witnesses so that testimony could be verified. He had two witnesses: himself and the Father (v. 18). But they immediately wanted to know where his father was so the testimony could be verified. They may have been Galileans who brought up the question of the legitimacy of his birth by that question. Or they may have been Judeans who did not know that but did want to see his father produced so the story could be checked.

In a statement that indicates an eyewitness, the Gospel writer noted that Jesus had been doing that teaching in the Court of the Women near the treasury boxes. That would have been close to the meeting place of the Sanhedrin. They could have heard what he said. They could have apprehended him. But they did not because his "hour," his time for presentation and glorification, had not yet come in God's time (v. 20).

But the time would come when Jesus would go away from them. They would not know where he had gone. Seeking him then, they would be unable to find him and also unable to join him (v. 21). Since they had rejected him when he was available to them, they would die in their sinful condition of rejection of the light of God's grace.

When Jesus had earlier mentioned his departure (7:33) they thought that perhaps he was going among the Dispersion. This time (v. 22) they wondered if he were contemplating suicide.

Again showing that they thought on different levels, Jesus observed that they could not understand his meaning because their way of thinking was completely earthbound while his way of thinking was heavenly (v. 23). They would die in their sins unless they believed on him (v. 24).

At this, they exclaimed, "Who are you?" (v. 25). Who was he to make that kind of claim? Jesus reiterated that he had told them all along who he was. He had come from the Father, and he had spoken the truth of the Father (v. 26). They did not understand his reference to the Father. But the time would come when he was lifted up by his death on the cross that they would know who he was, from whom he had come, and the truth of what he taught (v. 28). In all that he had done Jesus had been pleasing the Father who had sent him with his obedience. He was not alone; the Father was with him and in him (v. 29).

Many of those present believed on Jesus after this exchange. It is not clear whether the believers were from the bystanders or his antagonists, or perhaps some from each group (v. 30).

To those who had believed on him Jesus gave the condition of discipleship. They were true believers if they continued in his word (v. 31), if they would abide in and live by his teachings. Recognizing the superficiality of their belief he let them know that discipleship rested on obedience. There is a question about how those who believed on him in verse 30 and are described as believers in verse

31 could be charged with trying to kill Jesus in verse 37. Some find a distinction between "believed in him" in verse 30 and "believed him" (which does not show up clearly in the RSV translation) in verse 31. There is a difference in believing in what Jesus taught and in committing oneself to him in faith, believing in him. The distinction is in the superficiality of the belief of those who believed. They believed what he said; but they had not committed themselves in faith to him. That was what he emphasized.

Those who would abide in his word would know the truth. This truth would be liberating (v. 32). This is not simply a text for a library or a justification for a school. It is a spiritual truth that those who continue in faith in discipleship with Jesus will know the truth, God's truth which is God himself. God sets people free. The reference is to the liberation of salvation that comes from knowing God in faith through Jesus Christ.

The reference to freedom, however, turned their thoughts to political freedom rather than spiritual and emotional freedom. Boasting that they were descendants of Abraham, they claimed they had never been enslaved by anyone. They did not need liberation (v. 33). It is interesting that they would make the boast since they had been subjugated to other nations in the past and at that time were under the rule of Rome. Perhaps they were saying that they had never submitted themselves to other gods or that they had never willingly given in to other rulers.

Continuing his own line of reasoning Jesus said that the one who continually lived in sin, in contrast to the one who continually lived in his word, was a slave to sin. Sin made the choices for that person (v. 34). The slave had neither security nor permanency. There was no guarantee that he would spend his life with one family. In another contrast, Jesus showed that the son would always be a part of the family. The kind of liberation that he, the Son of God, would give would allow them to live as children of God in the family of God (v. 36). While they were physically descendants of Abraham, they had shown that they were not spiritually descendants of Abraham. Abraham was the father of faith. He followed God in faith. These people did not recognize the truth of God when it was spoken by Jesus who had received it from God (v. 38). They were showing family characteristics of another father, that one who sought to eliminate God's truth as they sought to eliminate Jesus.

Persisting in their claim of racial superiority, they again claimed Abraham as their father (v. 39). Jesus' observation is caught up in the popular saying, "Like father, like son." If they had truly been descended from Abraham they would act in faith as he did.

Pushing the question of paternity a step further, they claimed God as their Father (v. 41). Perhaps hinting at the questions surrounding the birth of Jesus they boasted that they were not born due to fornication. Ignoring that, Jesus responded to their claim of God as Father by saying that if God were their Father they would love him and believe him. Since he had come from God (v. 42) they should accept what God had sent him to do. The reasons they did not accept him and believe him was because they were behaving as the descendants of Satan rather than the descendants of God. Satan had from the very beginning been murderous and slanderous (v. 44). In trying to kill him and in refusing to believe him they were acting just like the devil. If they were of God they would accept him and his teachings (v. 47). As William Hull observed in the *Broadman Bible Commentary* the issue is not simply who a person *is* but who he *is of*. By their unbelief they were demonstrating that they were of the devil. But that did not have to be a permanent condition. By belief in Jesus Christ the devil's hold on them could be destroyed. It is a matter of one's own will.

Pushed to the wall by Jesus' logic, the Jews resorted to name calling (v. 48). First they called him a Samaritan. This could have referred to the mixed blood of the Samaritans, reflecting verse 41. Or perhaps it had reference to their thinking that he was picking and choosing which portions of the Scriptures he would follow as they thought the Samaritans did by not accepting the prophets. Then they said that he had a demon.

Ignoring the charge of being a Samaritan, which may have been a more demeaning name to them than to him, Jesus replied to the charge of demon possession. Jesus had said that they were of their father the devil. They had countered by saying that Jesus must be from the devil since he had a demon. Jesus insisted, though, that God would be the one who made the accurate judgment (v. 51). He did not seek to glorify himself, but only sought to glorify God, his Father.

Then he enunciated one of his claims. In solemn announcement he said that the one who kept his words would never know death

(v. 51). That convinced them that he was demon possessed. Abraham had died. The prophets had died. Was he claiming to be greater than both Abraham and the prophets? (v. 53).

But Jesus reminded them that he did not seek self-glorification. He only wanted to glorify the Father who had sent him. Him they called God. But they did not really know God. Jesus really knew God since he had come from him, and he would have been a liar to have said otherwise.

As far as Abraham was concerned, Abraham saw the day of Jesus and rejoiced (v. 56). By his "day" Jesus had reference to the entire incarnation event of his coming to the earth as a man, his death, and his resurrection. Taking it literally, they observed that Jesus was still a young man, not even qualifying as an elder at age fifty; he could not have seen Abraham who lived centuries earlier. In answer to that, Jesus said that he existed before Abraham ever existed (see 1:1).

And that upset them to the point that they picked up rocks to stone him. Jesus, however, was hid from them and left the Temple area. The sense is not that he cleverly escaped them but that God protected him in allowing him to get away from them.

Healing a Man Born Blind: The Light of Life (9:1-41)

Likely as Jesus left the Temple area (8:59) he and the disciples passed a man who had been born blind, presumably begging. The sight of this man prompted a question about the origin of evil and suffering. They asked whether the cause of this man's blindness was his own sin or his parent's sin. The Jewish people of the time had a rather simplistic explanation of evil. All evil came as a result of sin. The Book of Job notwithstanding, the notion persisted. To explain the man's condition of a congenital blindness, then, they had to resort to an idea of some kind of prenatal sin, or sin in a preexistent state, or of punishment for the sin of his parents. Having difficulty with the concept of how one could sin before he was born, they put the question to Jesus.

Refusing to be drawn into the argument about the origin of suffering, Jesus responded that it was not necessarily the result of either his sin or his parent's sin. All suffering is not always the direct result of sin. Rather than trying to fix blame for sin, the better part is to find opportunity for ministry. This Jesus did. The question about sin was less important than the fact that this man's misfortune could be turned into an opportunity to show the grace of God's work in a human life (v. 3).

Jesus then observed that both he and his followers must be alert to carry out the work of God in the daytime when work is normally done before the night comes when work cannot be done (v. 4). Too, there is an element of urgency about doing God's work. Echoing his claim in 8:12, Jesus said that he was the light of the world as long as he was in the world (v. 5). So the metaphor of day and night played into the contrast in John's Gospel between light and darkness. As the light of the world, Jesus came to dispel darkness. And he demonstrated it with this man.

Making a salve out of spit and clay Jesus put it on the man's eyes and told him to wash in the pool of Siloam (vv. 6-7). From Jesus came the means of healing, but the man had to be obedient to his word for the healing to take place. And the author added one of his interpretive remarks indicating that the translation of Siloam meant "sent." This was because the water was sent to the pool through a channel from the spring of Gihon. But to the writer of the Gospel it had deeper meaning. Jesus was the one sent from God to do the work of God. As this man was sent to the pool, the power of God was sent to his life by the One sent from God.

The man was cured of his blindness (v. 8). As he returned, now seeing, the people began to discuss his identity. Some thought that he was the blind beggar, while others thought that he must be someone who resembled the beggar. The man himself ended their confusion by identifying himself as the formerly blind beggar who now could see (v. 9). In answer to the next logical question as to how he became sighted he told them that the man called Jesus had given him instructions after anointing his eyes. The result was that he received his sight. But he confessed that he did not know where Jesus was when they asked him that next question (v. 12).

The newly-sighted man was carried to the Pharisees either on the day he was healed or on the next day (v. 13). The Pharisees could see a problem with the healing. It had been done on a sabbath. Besides, in making the salve of spit and clay Jesus had worked on a sabbath. To their way of thinking, no one could truly be from God who so disregarded their interpretation of the sabbath. That the pitiful man had been healed at the first opportunity, indicating that Jesus worked the works of God when he could (v. 4), did not impress them. That he did it on the sabbath concerned them.

When asked how he was healed the man gave a straightforward testimony to Jesus (v. 15). This testimony caused a division in the ranks of the Pharisees. One group was convinced that Jesus could not have been from God and disregarded the sabbath. The other group was convinced that what Jesus did proved what he was. They were sure a sinner could not do such things (v. 16). That latter group apparently was overwhelmed by the former group, since the course of moderation concerning Jesus was not followed.

With a division in their ranks, the Pharisees asked the man who was most familiar with the work of Jesus for his opinion of him. Giving him probably the highest spiritual designation he could imagine, the man said that Jesus was a prophet (v. 17). This was a further step in his understanding of Christ since he had earlier identified him as simply a man (v. 11).

Attempting to discredit the healing, the Pharisees, now identified by the more common designation of "Jews," called the man's parents as the next step (v. 18). They asked them two questions: was this their son who had been born blind? and how was he healed? (v. 10). They could answer the first question easily enough. That was their son who had been blind all of his life. But they would not touch the second question. They professed not to know how he was healed. Since he was of legal age to give testimony, the Jews could ask him themselves if they wanted to know (v. 21).

The reason for the parent's strange reaction was that the Jewish leaders had already decided that anyone confessing Jesus as the Messiah would be excommunicated from the synagogue (v. 22). While this was probably a temporary withdrawal of religious privileges, it was enough to frighten the parents. It could also have been a rather informal decision among some of the leaders that had leaked out to the people.

Calling the man before them the second time, which would suggest a formal inquiry, they commanded him to give God the glory and to admit that Jesus was a sinner (v. 24). To give God the glory was a call for a frank, unadorned answer given as an oath. As to Jesus, their mind was already made up: he was a sinner.

The man did not feel qualified to judge whether Jesus was a sinner. But he had an honest witness he could give to Jesus: he had been blind; now he could see (v. 25). No more eloquent witness could have been given. And no more convincing testimony could be considered.

They wanted to know once more how it had been done. Getting aggravated at their insistence, the man responded that he had already told them all of that. He sarcastically asked if the reason they wanted to hear it again was that they wanted to become his disciples (v. 27).

This answer caused them to abuse the man verbally. With pride they boasted that they followed Moses. Speaking contemptuously of Jesus, they asserted that they did not know where he had come from.

The formerly blind man used solid theological logic in his amazement that they did not know where Jesus came from. They were supposed to be theologically aware. Jesus gave him sight. Their theology presupposed that God would not listen to and thus work through anyone who did not obey him. Jesus had healed him. From the previous record (the Old Testament) there was no account of a person giving sight to a blind person. Therefore, Jesus must have been from God or he could not have healed the man (vv. 30-33).

Having been bested in theological logic, they resorted to accusations and name-calling. They were offended that this one whom they charged had been born in utter sin—perhaps a reference to the reason for his being blind in the first place (v. 2)—would try to teach them something about God. So they cast him out of the synagogue. What his parents feared for themselves was experienced by their son.

When Jesus heard what had happened to the man he looked him up (v. 35). Upon finding him, Jesus asked him one decisive question: "Do you believe in the Son of man?" (v. 35).

Remember that the man had not seen Jesus since his healing. Perhaps he recognized the voice. His answer to Jesus was another question. He wanted to know the identity of the Son of man, which he understood as a reference to the Messiah. If he knew him he would believe on him (v. 36). Jesus then identified himself to the man by saying that the man had seen the Messiah sent from God. In fact, he was speaking to him at that moment (v. 37).

Upon this revelation, the man confessed, "Lord, I believe" (v. 38) and worshiped Jesus. This is the only reference in the Fourth Gospel to a person worshiping Jesus. His faith in Jesus had become complete. He confessed him as Lord and worshiped him.

A progression in this man's faith can be followed. He first called Jesus simply a man who did amazing things (v. 11). From that he went on to designate Jesus as a prophet (v. 17). Then he identified him as one sent from God (v. 33). And, in full faith, he called him "Lord"—indicating his belief that Jesus was the Messiah, the Son of man, the One sent from God who should be worshiped. This man had come from darkness into the light, both literally and spiritually.

Jesus remarked publicly that his coming into the world brought a judgment to the world (v. 39). By his coming into the world those who did not see gain sight while those who see are blind. Realizing that he was talking about them, the Pharisees who overheard his remark asked if that meant that they were blind. They probably expected him to answer affirmatively and would thus have had further reason to oppose him.

Instead, Jesus answered that they would be better off if they were blind. If they were blind they would not be guilty for failing to have the spiritual insight to see him for what he really was. But since they professed to have sight, to see, they stood guilty and condemned for willful blindness. The problem was not one of honest doubt but of such self-satisfied prejudice that they refused to see the light (v. 41). Jesus is the light of the world who leads to life. Those are condemned who refuse to see his light.

Talking About the Good Shepherd: The Shepherd of Life (10:1-42)

Having been cast out of the synagogue, the man who had been cured of his blindness by Jesus was a sheep out of the sheepfold, so to speak. But Jesus had found him, gathered him to himself, and made him a part of his flock through the man's faith in Jesus. Since it follows directly after the incident concerning the blind man who was given sight, the discourse about the good shepherd has to be related to that. The passage is understood better with that experience in the background and is, therefore, not just an unrelated discourse. Some of the Old Testament references to rulers and leaders as shepherds, particularly Ezekiel 34 and Isaiah 56:9-12 as well as the beloved Psalm 23, should also be kept in mind with this passage.

In Judea especially, where shepherding was a part of life, the people were familiar with the sheepfold. It was something like a pen, often constructed of rocks or limbs and even sometimes a cave.

In some cases it stood in front of the house in which the shepherd lived and its entrance was also the entrance to the house. Some pens were partially roofed, and others were entirely open to the air. A gatekeeper or porter could be employed at night to watch the sheepfold.

In a solemn announcement, "Truly, truly," Jesus observed that the shepherd could openly walk into the sheepfold by the door. The thief who came by stealth or the robber who came by violence would find some other way of entry. When the shepherd appeared, the gatekeeper would allow him in. The sheep would hear and recognize his voice and would follow him. The presence and the voice of another would cause the sheep to panic (vv. 1-5).

This little story is as close as the Fourth Gospel gets to the parables of Jesus found in the Synoptic Gospels. In fact, it is variously called a parable, a proverb, or a "figure" (RSV). Obviously, it has some allegorical characteristics, even though it is not quite accurate to call it an allegory. The reference has to be to Jesus as the Good Shepherd sent from God to gather to himself those who belong to God by faith. Others attempt to lead away or to steal away the flock of God by violence or by stealth. But those who have responded to the voice of God can hear the voice of God in the one sent from God and follow him.

As was often true of the parables of Jesus, the ones who heard it did not comprehend its meaning (v. 6). They had not followed the leader God had sent to them and could not hear his voice.

Since the people did not understand the little parable Jesus gave them, he interpreted it for them. In his interpretation he used two metaphors to describe himself: "the door" (vv. 7,9) and the "good shepherd" (vv. 11,14). Each would have symbolic meaning to those who first heard it.

The sheepfold often would not have a regular door, only an opening. At night the shepherd would lie across that opening. That way he could control the entrance into the sheepfold. No sheep would get out without his knowing it; no marauder could get in without his being aware of it. Jesus, in another of his "I am" claims, claimed to be the door.

In verse 8 Jesus indicated that he regulated the shepherds that entered the fold. Verse 9 shows that he regulated the entrance and exit of the sheep between fold and pasture. Jesus, then, would decide both about the sheep and the shepherd, both the ministry and the membership of the church. Entrance into the family of God is gained through Jesus Christ alone.

Those who had come before him were characterized as thieves and robbers who destroyed and scattered rather than saved and unified the flock. Obviously, this could not apply to all the prophets and spiritual leaders such as Moses. It could well apply, however, to those unqualified spiritual leaders referred to in Ezekiel 34 and Isaiah 56, as well as the current religious leadership that was rather self-serving. Most of the leaders of first-century Judaism were more concerned with their own position and power than with the flock. There could also be a reference to the false messiahs that had risen up from time to time but who did not attract a following among the people.

As the only entrance into the family of God, Jesus gave salvation, security, and satisfaction to all who came into the kingdom of God through faith in him (v. 9). That is in contrast to the false leaders whose results are disastrous. They brought death; Jesus brought life (v. 10). And the life that he brought to all those who believed on him was an abundant, full, meaningful kind of life.

Then he changed the metaphor to that of the good shepherd (v. 11). Jesus added one thing to the popular image of the good shepherd: the good shepherd would lay down his life for his sheep. This characteristic of the sacrificial shepherd who willingly laid down his life for his sheep was repeated five times in this section. He would give guidance and protection and sustenance, even at the cost of his own life.

The contrast here is between the good shepherd who willingly risks his life for the sheep and the day laborer who is interested only in his wages (vv. 11-12). Since he does not have the pride of possession, when danger comes he leaves. More interested in saving his own skin than in saving the sheep, he leaves them to the marauding wolf who scatters the flock as he kills some sheep. The day laborer does not have personal concern for the sheep.

Not so with the good shepherd. Not only is he concerned about his sheep, he knows them individually and personally. He knows them and they know him, just as he is known by the Father and intimately knows the Father (v. 15).

Jesus had other sheep also than those who were the Jews of his day. Whereas Judaism was exclusive, Christianity was inclusive. The initial ministry of Jesus was aimed at the lost sheep of the house of Israel (Matt. 15:24), but in the end it would reach out to the Gentiles and to the ends of the earth. These folks, too, would be gathered into the one sheepfold of faith under the guidance of the one good shepherd, the Christ himself (v. 16).

In a reference to his predicted death and resurrection, Jesus indicated that the Father loved him and approved of him because of his obedience in laying down his life (v. 17). His sacrificial death was his voluntary choice. He had the power to lay down his life willingly for others, and through this power his life would be taken up again. He would be obedient to the Father and operate in the Father's power that was shared with him (v. 18).

Jesus' statements about intimacy with the Father always brought a reaction. It brought the same reaction as before, as "again" (v. 19) the people were divided over their appreciation of Jesus. Some charged him with demon possession, which they equated with madness. It is interesting that the only references to demon possession in the Fourth Gospel are in relation to the charges against Jesus that he was possessed by a demon or his defense from that charge. Other people, however, could not get over the works of wonder that he had done. They were convinced that one who could open the eyes of the blind (refer to ch. 9) could not be possessed by a demon (v. 21). But no progress was made among the people. They divided into the same two groups who questioned or supported him. What he wanted was for them to believe on him.

A time reference is given to indicate that the next discussion of Jesus with the Jewish leaders was at the Feast of Dedication (v. 22). This was a winter (November/December) feast celebrating the rededication of the Temple by Judas Maccabaeus in 165 BC, following its profanation by Antiochus Epiphanes. About three months after the Feast of the Tabernacles, it was celebrated in much the same way. Sometimes called the Festival of Lights, it is known today as Hanukkah.

Apparently, then, about three months after the previous discourse in which Jesus had given the little parable on the sheep and the shepherds Jesus was back in Jerusalem. This time it does not seem that he was formally teaching but was on the portico or colonnaded porch on the east of the Temple known as Solomon's portico. The Jews approached him and asked for a direct and simple answer as to whether he were the Christ (v. 24).

Jesus answered that he had already told them that but they did not believe (v. 25). While he had made his identity known to both the Samaritan woman at the well (4:26) and to the man born blind (9:35), he had never plainly said to the Jews that he was the Christ. Their messianic expectations and his understanding of his messianic mission were so different that a plain affirmative answer would have been misleading. But the drift of his teachings, his claim of unity with the Father, and the mighty works he had done all would have pointed to that if they had believed on him rather than shutting him out (v. 25).

Jesus went on to say that they did not believe because they did not belong (v. 26). His sheep would hear his voice and recognize it as the authentic voice of God. In following him they would know him for what he was, and he would know them personally. The result was that through his grace he would give to them eternal life, a never-ending life with the quality of eternity about it. Those who come to him by faith have been given to him by the Father. No one can snatch them out of his hand nor the Father's hand. The believer has that kind of security (v. 29). The reason is because of the unity between Jesus, the Son, and God, the Father (v. 30). That unity reflects the words of the Prologue (1:1); they both are separate, but they both are an inseparable one (v. 30). With the Feast of Dedication in the background, Jesus showed complete dedication to the will of God.

For this claim of unity with the Father they were ready to stone him. Calling his statements blasphemy, they were acting as judge and jury to take the judgment in their own hand against blasphemy (Lev. 24:16). Always the calmest one in the face of personal danger, Jesus asked them for which of his works of grace they were going to stone him (v. 31). Their answer was that they would execute him for blasphemy, not for any of the works he had done.

Jesus then answered them with two lines of argument. The first argument answered the question of blasphemy directly. In Psalm 82:6, their own Scripture, which by their standards had to stand, mere men had been called gods. These persons had received the word of God. He was the Word of God. If these persons could be called gods it would certainly stand to reason that it was not blasphemous for the very Son of God to be identified since he had been dedicated by the Father and sent into the world by him (vv. 34-36).

The second argument had to do with his works, what he had done. They had seen the works and had admitted their authenticity. If they could not believe his words, surely they could believe his works. They were done in the power of the Father and in obedience to the Father. These works were sufficient to lead them both to know and understand that he was in the Father and the Father was in him (v. 38). They worked in concert. There was a mutual indwelling. Both by insight and by continued understanding the works should have been seen as the works of the Father.

Again they tried to arrest him (v. 30). But again, because his "hour" had not yet come, Jesus eluded them. He who was in the hands of God had escaped the hands of the arresters.

Leaving Jerusalem, Jesus went eastward across the Jordan River to the place where John the Baptist had baptized earlier (v. 40). There he stayed for awhile, likely the three-month period from the Feast of Dedication in December until the Feast of the Passover in March.

While on the other side of the Jordan he was not idle. Many people came to hear him there. John the Baptist had done no signs, had performed no miracles. But what he had said about Jesus was found to be true. Jesus enjoyed a good reception in that area. In the place where he had been baptized by John the Baptist, and where John the Baptist had prepared for his coming, a great number of people believed on Jesus (v. 42). Their response was in marked contrast to the response of the people in Jerusalem who had tried on several occasions to either arrest him or stone him or both.

Rejection (11:1 to 12:50)

Jesus had revealed himself to the world (chs. 2—4). People had reacted to him by faith and by rejection (chs. 5—10). The last part of the first half of John's Gospel (chs. 10—11) shows the rejection of Jesus by the religious leaders. His public ministry is presented in the series of signs along with the discourses (chs. 2—12).

Raising Lazarus from the Dead: The Lord of Life (11:1-54)

The seventh sign found in the Gospel of John is the raising of Lazarus from the dead. Martha, Mary, and Lazarus were a family for whom Jesus had deep affection. They lived at Bethany, which was just east of Jerusalem on the southeast slope of the Mount of Olives. The sisters, Mary and Martha, show up in the Synoptic Gospels, although Lazarus is mentioned only in John's Gospel. And, strangely enough, since the writer of the Fourth Gospel put so much significance on the raising of Lazarus from the dead, the miracle does not appear in the other Gospels.

Jesus was still east of the Jordan River when the word came to him that his friend Lazarus was sick. He was identified as the brother of Mary and Martha, all of whom lived in Bethany. Mary (v. 2) was further identified as the one who anointed the feet of Jesus with ointment and wiped them dry with her hair, anticipating an event recorded in the following chapter (12:1-8). Their message to Jesus was that the one whom he loved was sick (v. 3). Although the message had implicit in it a request to come to Bethany, the invitation was not explicitly stated. Jesus remarked, as he had concerning the man born blind (9:3), that the ultimate result of this illness would be the glory of God and the glorification of the Son of man (v. 4). While Lazarus did die from the illness, it was not a final, irrevocable death. Jesus did restore him to life. The term "glorification" was used by the writer of John's Gospel to refer to the hour of Jesus' glory when through his death and resurrection his true purpose was made known. This, too, would be a result of Lazarus's illness and subsequent restoration to life by Jesus (see 11:43).

Inexplicably, Jesus delayed going to Lazarus for two days after receiving the message (v. 6). Probably he knew that Lazarus would die before he could get there. Likely, also, he wanted it known that he went at his own initiative and not at the prompting of others, as with his first refusal to act at the wedding in Cana (2:4) and the healing of the nobleman's son (4:46-50). After waiting two days Jesus indicated that he was ready to go to Judea again (v. 7).

The disciples balked at a return to Judea. They reminded him that the Jewish leaders had tried to execute him by stoning the last time he was there (v. 8). But Jesus reminded them with a proverbial-type saying that one could walk in the twelve hours of daylight without stumbling, due to the light of the sun which functioned as the light of the world. But the one who walked in the darkness could easily stumble due to the darkness (v. 10). What he meant was that he had to work while he had the opportunity. There may also be a play on the words "light of this world" (v. 9), since Jesus had previously claimed to be the "light of the world" (8:12). As Jesus followed the light of the leadership of God he had to go back. By his return the Light of the world would shed illumination on the nature of death and the power of God.

Jesus then explained that Lazarus had fallen asleep and he had to go wake him from his sleep (v. 11). Taking him literally, the disciples observed that if he slept then he would recover soon. The sleep would be good for him (v. 12). But Jesus meant that he had died. For the follower of Jesus Christ death is like a sleep; death has lost its note of finality. Jesus repeated it plainly enough that they could understand him: Lazarus was dead (v. 14). He then went on to explain that he was glad that Lazarus was dead for their sakes. What they would experience in the raising of Lazarus from the dead would be more significant as they realized without doubt that Lazarus was dead. They would believe when they knew he was dead (v. 15).

In a note of resignation that also indicated the depth of his commitment to Christ, Thomas suggested that they go along with Jesus so they could die with him. Known as the Twin, Thomas showed more courage and faith than he is often given credit (v. 16).

By the time Jesus and his disciples reached Bethany Lazarus had been dead for four days (v. 17). Assuming that the messengers came to Jesus in one day, and he tarried two more days before starting to Bethany, and the trip to Bethany took a day, the four days are counted from the time Jesus got the message. He could not have reached Bethany before Lazarus's death if he had left immediately. The notation that Bethany was about two miles from Jerusalem explained both the number of mourners present and the speed with which the raising of Lazarus from the dead was known by the Jewish leaders.

Upon hearing that Jesus was approaching, Martha left the house to meet him while Mary remained in the house (v. 20). Martha's greeting to Jesus—"Lord, if you had been here, my brother would not have died" (v. 21)—may have been a rebuke, or it simply could have been an expression of regret. Possibly Martha and Mary had said the same thing to one another often over the past four days.

But then she followed that greeting with an affirmation of faith: "And even now I know that whatsoever you ask from God, God will give you" (v. 22). What did she want him to ask from God? Did she expect Jesus to raise her brother from the dead? Probably not. When they went to the tomb later it was Martha who protested the removal of the stone from the door that sealed the tomb (v. 39). Probably she was expressing the confidence that whatever she needed in comfort, strength, help, and hope God could provide for her through Jesus Christ. Probably she got more from God through Christ than she expected when her brother was raised from the dead.

Jesus assured her that her brother would rise again (v. 23). To that she responded that she knew that he would rise again at the general resurrection. The Pharisees and most pious Jews believed in a resurrection. Perhaps this had been given to her repeatedly as an expression of comfort and hope since her brother's death. Her response to Jesus indicated that perhaps she thought Jesus was just repeating to her what others had already said by way of comfort.

Jesus, however, meant more than that. In one of the most significant of his claims in the Gospel of John he said, "I am the resurrection and the life" (v. 25). Both resurrection and life are centered in Jesus Christ. A resurrection in the last days is not just a vague hope. In Jesus Christ it is reality. By his own resurrection from the dead he gave validity to the claim. What he claimed, he could do. He was resurrection himself. He brought resurrection to Lazarus. But he was also life. Life is defined in Jesus Christ. Standing there in the very presence of death Jesus claimed that life was his. He had come to give an eternal life that even death could not snatch away.

He explained further what he meant by resurrection and life—that a person who believes in Jesus Christ personally shall continue to live, though he were to die physically. The one who lives through belief in Jesus Christ shall never die (v. 26). Physical death may overtake the believer, but spiritual death has no power over him. And all of this is possible through Jesus Christ. In Christ the last days had already arrived. Eternity had invaded time. Death may stand before one as the last enemy and the strongest enemy. But even that enemy is defeated through belief in Jesus Christ. In Christ is both resurrection and life.

Pointedly, Jesus asked Martha, "Do you believe this?" (v. 26). No one can sidestep the directness of that question. Each one has to answer it; and each one has to answer it personally.

Martha's answer was a threefold profession of faith in Jesus Christ. Her answer affirmed that she believed that he was the Christ, the Messiah that God would send into the world. Not only that, she believed he was the Son of God. And added to that was her belief that he was the one God had promised to send into the world to deliver the world (v. 27). That was a firm and clear confession of Christ.

Although it is not recorded in the Gospel, Jesus apparently asked to see Mary. Martha went to the house and told Mary that Jesus, whom she called the "Teacher," was there and asking for her (v. 28). Possibly Martha meant to stay with the guests who had come to offer their condolences as Mary had stayed inside with the mourners when Martha met Jesus outside the village (v. 28). Seeing Mary arising quickly to go to Jesus, the Jewish people who had come to mourn with them thought that she was going to the grave to weep and followed her out of the house (v. 31). Instead, Mary went to the place outside the village of Bethany where Martha had met Jesus earlier. The mourners were with her.

Falling at the feet of Jesus, Mary repeated what Martha had said earlier. If Jesus had only been there he could have healed Lazarus from his illness and kept him from dying (v. 32). She added no more to that judgment. But by calling him "Lord" she expressed her faith in him and put herself at his disposal.

Jesus was deeply moved at her grief and her implicit trust in him (v. 33). The presence of the Jews there who added to the scene with their loud wailing as expressions of grief also added to his inner turmoil. When he asked where they had buried Lazarus (v. 34), they replied by asking him to come and see the place. At this Jesus wept (v. 35). He wept because of his deep love and affection for Lazarus and his sisters Martha and Mary. But very likely he also wept because of his deep burden at what this would cost him. If he did what he had come to do in giving life to Lazarus he knew that it would mean the giving up of his life. Some have found in this deep turmoil of the Master, expressed by his weeping, another version of

Jesus' agony in the Garden of Gethsemane prior to his crucifixion. From John's account this event was what sealed his doom. Jesus also could have been deeply troubled by the misunderstanding of the people concerning death and the life that he would give. What Jesus would do in raising his friend from the dead would be at great personal cost.

Even at the grave site the people were divided in their reaction to Jesus. Some of them noted how deeply he loved Lazarus (v. 36), interpreting his tears as a genuine expression of sorrow. Others remarked that since he could have healed the blind man he surely could have kept his friend from death (v. 37). Perhaps those who refused to believe Jesus found fault in his refusal to help Lazarus.

Arriving at the tomb, which was apparently a cave in a hillside with a stone covering the entrance, Jesus was again moved emotionally (v. 38). Summoning the help of others, he asked for the stone to be moved. At this Martha protested that her brother had been dead and buried four days already; decomposition would have begun (v. 39). The Jewish people believed that the spirit of a dead person hovered over the body for three days and departed by the fourth day when the process of decomposition would have begun. There could be no doubt on the part of any who witnessed the scene that Lazarus was actually dead. At that, Jesus reminded her of something he had told her at some earlier date. If she would but believe she would see the glory of God (v. 40). Apparently they were still not expecting a resurrection. What they would see in their belief in the power of God through Jesus would indeed bring glory to God.

They moved the stone. Jesus prayed. His prayer was a prayer of thanksgiving that the Father had heard him (v. 41). It was not for his sake that he offered this prayer of thanksgiving. He knew that the Father always heard him; but the prayer was for the sake of those who observed the event. Coming on the heels of his prayer they could not help realizing that it was the power of God that brought Lazarus back to life, not the trickery of a wonder worker (v. 42).

Then in a loud voice, addressing him by name, Jesus called, "Lazarus, come out" (v. 43). And he did. Still bound in the graveclothes, which were strips of cloth wrapped around him with a handkerchief-type covering over the face, Lazarus came out. Jesus then told them to unbind him and let him loose. This was done

(v. 44). Lazarus had been raised from the dead! The one who had claimed to be both resurrection and life had provided both resurrection and life to one of his followers. This was a demonstration, a dramatic presentation, of the power of God in Jesus Christ to do exactly what Christ had promised to do.

As usually happened, this event caused a division among the people. Some of them believed on Jesus (v. 45). They were among those who had come with Mary from the house to meet Jesus. Overwhelmed by the witness that God had acted decisively in Jesus, they believed. But others did not believe. And those unbelieving ones ran straight to the Pharisees to report what had happened (v. 46). They could not refute the miracle. That had been verified. What they did refute was the larger testimony that Jesus had been sent from God and that he acted in the power of God.

With this news, the Pharisees and the chief priests who were Sadducees called together an informal meeting of the council, the Sanhedrin, which was the ruling body of the Jews (v. 47). The purpose of the meeting was to decide what to do about Jesus. He was doing so many signs and was convincing so many people that they were concerned about the people following him. This concern had two prongs. On the one hand, if what Jesus taught about God and his relationship with God was right, they were wrong. The collapse of their whole system could follow a wholesale turning to Jesus. On the other hand, if the people believed Jesus and the messianic expectations began to run too high, there might be the kind of disturbance that would bring in the Roman authorities. The Romans allowed them free rein in matters of religion unless trouble broke out. If trouble occurred, the Romans would move in quickly. In that case, they would lose their privileged position. At the bottom, self-interest was evident in each line of argument (v. 48).

Speaking very haughtily, Caiaphas, whom the writer noted was the high priest that fateful year, said that they knew nothing at all. He would tell them exactly what should be done and how it should be done. Speaking from the standpoint of expediency, without regard for right or wrong or the revelation of God, it would be better for one man to die than for the whole nation to die (v. 50). This was a politically-motivated statement. As he expressed it, Caiaphas had no spiritual intent in mind. He was noting that it would be better for them to offer Jesus as a sacrifice, to put him to death, so that the

Romans would not move in to extinguish the nation as they knew it. From that perspective the death of Jesus would save the nation from extinction.

The writer of the Fourth Gospel, however, gave a theological interpretation to Caiaphas' political statement. He said that God had directed him to say more than he meant to say. By Jesus' death on the cross he would save that nation. But not only that nation would be saved; Christ would bring salvation to all the people who believed on God through him wherever those people were scattered. The universal nature of the gospel was noted. By his death on the cross Jesus was providing salvation for all (v. 52).

From that time the fate of Jesus was sealed. The argument of Caiaphas based on self-interest and expediency carried the day. From that time that Jesus would have to die was decided. All that was not decided was how it would be done and when it would happen (v. 54). From the perspective of the writer of John's Gospel the raising of Lazarus from the dead was the final act that sealed the doom of Jesus. Jesus had said that he would lay down his life. But the Jewish authorities were determined to take his life.

This also brought to a close the public ministry of Jesus. The Passover would occur shortly after this event. And that Passover would occasion the death of Jesus. Since the Sanhedrin had already decided that Jesus must die, he did not minister openly among them. That would invite death. With his disciples he went to Ephraim which was in the wilderness area about twelve to fifteen miles from Jerusalem and stayed until the Passover season (v. 54).

Preparing for the Passover: A Plot Against Life (11:55-57)

The third Passover mentioned by John (2:13; 6:4) helps to give the framework for a three-year ministry by Jesus. The major religious festival of the Jewish people, the Passover, brought many people to Jerusalem from many areas, even areas outside Palestine. Since they would often have been religiously contaminated by contact with Gentiles they spent some time in ritual purification. This would often take a week (v. 55).

As the people gathered they questioned whether Jesus would come. They knew the danger to his life, for the religious authorities had already put out an order for people to report his presence so they could arrest him (v. 57). Jesus' life was in danger.

Anointing the Feet of Jesus: Preparation for His Death (12:1-11)

The countdown to the cross had begun. The decision had been solidified that Jesus must die (11:53). As the Passover approached, the people were interested in whether Jesus would be present (11:56), and the Jewish authorities had given instructions that he should be reported if sighted (11:57). The writer of John's Gospel dated the death of Jesus to coincide with the slaughter of the lamb at Passover. So the dating of the supper in his honor would have to be Saturday evening following the sabbath (v. 1).

Prior to the Passover Jesus went to Bethany. While there he was treated to a supper in his honor on the Saturday before Passover. The site of the supper is not mentioned, but it is presumed to have been at the home of Lazarus, Martha, and Mary since Martha is mentioned as serving and Mary as anointing the feet of Jesus with the costly perfume. Lazarus was at the table.

During the course of the meal Mary took a pound (actually about twelve ounces, more like a pint) of a costly perfume called nard and poured it over the feet of Jesus (v. 3). She poured so much on his feet that she wiped up the excess with her hair. So pungent was the smell of the perfume that the whole house was filled with its aroma (v. 3).

All four Gospels have an account of the anointing of Jesus with expensive ointment by a woman (Matt. 26:6-13; Mark 14:3-9; Luke 7:36-50). But all of them differ in details. John placed it before the triumphal entry of Sunday and Mark after it. Matthew and Mark also locate it in Bethany but put the supper at the home of Simon the Leper. They also record that the ointment was poured on his head as though to anoint a king while John and the anointing in Luke have it poured on Jesus' feet. Only John named the woman who anointed Jesus while Luke indicated that she was a sinner. The sinful woman in Luke's account used her hair to wipe away the tears that had fallen on the feet of Jesus before she anointed the feet. These differences have led interpreters to understand them as variations of the same event, two different events with the sinful woman and with Mary at Bethany, or Mary's act as an independent action. If taken as an independent action, Mary's act of devotion to the Lord showed some differences. Jesus would have been reclining at the table with his feet exposed. The anointing of the feet would have been similar to a servant's washing the feet of a guest upon arrival. But Mary also wiped away the excess perfume with her hair, showing further humility, since Jewish women of good reputation did not usually allow their hair to hang loose. Such was her devotion to the Christ and her humility before him that she would anoint the humblest part of his body, the feet, and wipe them with the most glorious part of her body (1 Cor. 11:15), her hair.

But all of those present did not see it as an act of devotion and humility. Judas Iscariot griped about it. The story of Judas' betrayal of Jesus is anticipated as Judas Iscariot is identified both as a disciple and as the betrayer (v. 4). He wanted to know why the expensive perfume was not sold and the money given to the poor (v. 5). Why, that much perfume could have been sold for three hundred denarii. That was quite a sum of money. A denarius was a silver coin that was equal to a day's wage for a laboring man. That would equate almost a year's work for the common laborer.

A further insight into Judas' character is given with the observation that Judas did not protest because he was concerned with the poor but because he was greedy for the money. He was the treasurer of the apostolic band and would sometimes pilfer money from their common treasury (v. 6).

Jesus, however, supported Mary in her act of devotion (v. 7). What she had done was in preparation for his burial. There is a contrast in the attitude of Mary and the attitude of the disciples. She was sensitive enough to anoint his body and thus to honor him before his death. The others were so insensitive that all they could consider was the cost of the ointment. In all probability Mary was not aware that her act of anointing Jesus was a prior preparation for his burial. She would have no way of knowing that his death would occur just prior to the sabbath and that they would not have the opportunity for proper preparation of the body before burial (19:39-40). She was so grateful to Jesus for restoring her brother to life, and so aware of the cost to him personally of that act, that she rather spontaneously anointed his feet. Jesus interpreted that as her prior preparation of his body for burial.

Quoting Deuteronomy 15:11, Jesus went on to say that the poor would always be there for ministry (v. 8). If one were really interested in ministering to the poor one would have no lack of opportunity. But the ministry of devotion and gratitude that would be performed for him would have to be done quickly. He would not always be there. In fact, his time of life on earth was short.

This statement does not represent callousness on Jesus' part. Nor does it indicate the hopelessness of trying to alleviate poverty. It is not a proof text against social action. It is, instead, the observation that the opportunity for ministry and devotion must be seized while it is available. They could honor Jesus at that time. In a very short while they would not be able to honor him.

When the word reached nearby Jerusalem that Jesus was at Bethany great crowds of people went there (v. 9). They came to see Jesus who would be famous as a fugitive and to look at Lazarus who would be viewed somewhat as a freak since he had been raised from the dead. The chief priests were Sadducees who did not believe in the resurrection. The presence of Lazarus alive and well was particularly embarrassing to them. So the decision was made that not only would Jesus have to be put to death but that Lazarus must die also (v. 10). The continued presence of Lazarus would lend credence to the power of Jesus and thus increase his popularity. Already many of the Jewish people were expressing belief in Jesus because of Lazarus as proof of his power (v. 11).

Entering Jerusalem: The Triumphal Entry (12:12-19)

With a time reference back to verse 1 the writer sets the stage for Jesus' triumphal entry into Jerusalem (v. 12). The crowd that heard that Jesus was coming to the feast was likely composed of many Galileans, among whom Jesus' ministry had been very well received.

As Jesus approached Jerusalem, the people went out to meet him. As they went they took palm branches which were symbols of victory and waving them cried out, "Hosanna! Blessed be he who comes in the name of the Lord, even the King of Israel!" (v. 13). "Hosanna" means "Save now." They followed that with a quotation from Psalm 118:26. They added the part about the king of Israel. Obviously, the crowd, caught up in the excitement of Jesus' coming into Jerusalem, understood him as the coming one promised by God. Messianic expectations ran high. Jesus was beginning to fulfill them in the eyes of the crowd. They could understand a deliverer sent from God only as a king.

Jesus was interested in correcting their understanding of the Messiah, the coming one. Purposely finding a donkey, an ass, he rode it into the city. In doing that he carried out the prophecy of Zechariah 9:9 (v. 15). A king entering a city on an ass was a sign of peace. Had he come on a prancing stallion it would have been a symbol of war. Jesus came in peace to conquer the hearts of persons by love and belief.

The disciples did not really understand all of that at the time that it happened. In one of his editorial and explanatory comments the Gospel writer remarked that the disciples understood neither the incident nor the symbolism until after Jesus' glorification—his death, resurrection, and ascension (v. 16). Then under the guidance of the Holy Spirit they understood what it had meant.

Apparently two crowds are in mind in verses 17 and 18. One was the crowd of people who had witnessed the raising of Lazarus from the dead. The other crowd was the crowd of people in Jerusalem for the feast. The convergence of the two crowds would indicate that people from throughout the country were turning out to welcome Jesus. The Judean crowd witnessed to his raising of Lazarus from the dead. This excited the interest of the other people who were interested in seeing one who could do such a thing.

All of this served to raise the anxiety level of the Pharisees (v. 20). As they saw the people clamoring after Jesus they had the impression that everyone had turned to him. They felt that there was nothing that they could then do to stop him or to stem the tide of his popularity.

Inquiring About Jesus: the Greeks (12:20-26)

The Pharisees had been under the impression that the whole world was turning to Jesus (v. 19). As though to indicate that it was, John introduced the Greeks who wanted an interview with Jesus (v. 20). These could have been God-fearers who had some belief in God but had not become Jewish proselytes, or they could have been proselytes, although this probably would have been noted. It is also possible that they were Gentiles who were in Jerusalem at the time of the feast and were attracted to Jesus. That they were called Greeks simply indicates that they were not Jews. A lot of people from around the Mediterranean world were present for the Feast of Passover.

Why they came to Philip with their request to see Jesus is not clear. Philip is a Greek name. And he was from Bethsaida which was a rather Gentile city just outside Galilee on the east side of the Jordan River where it flows into the Sea of Galilee. Perhaps they felt an affinity to him. But Philip then sought the help of Andrew. Andrew, it seems, was in the habit of introducing people to Jesus (1:42; 6:8). Andrew, too, is a Greek name. When these Greeks wanted to see Jesus it implied more than just looking at him. They could have seen him walking around the area. They were, instead, interested in interviewing him, getting to know him. Andrew and Philip together went to Jesus with the request (v. 22).

There is no indication that Jesus directly addressed the Greeks who had wanted to see him. Rather, as he began to speak it probably was a general statement addressed to Philip and Andrew who were there, the Greeks who had come with them, and anyone else who happened to be within earshot. He began by saying that the hour had come when the Son of Man would be glorified (v. 23). Throughout his ministry he had pointed to that "hour" when he would be glorified. The "hour" indicated a special kind of time in which it would be made known who he was and why he had come into the world. The glorification by which this would be known was the event of the crucifixion, resurrection, and ascension. That time had come. That it had universal significance was seen in the presence of Gentiles there as well as Jews. His salvation was for all.

Then he indicated something of the nature of his glorification which would be the revelation of himself and his mission to the world. When a grain of wheat is planted it has to die to itself before it can come to new life in a plant (v. 24). Then it will bear fruit. He would have to die also before he would come to life through the resurrection and bring about the fruit of new life to those who believed on him. A person can value life too highly. A person who is so self-seeking in his own life that he selfishly holds it to himself will end up losing it (v. 25). That is a self-defeating kind of life. But the person who is willing to give up his life for others will discover that he has found true life. That is exactly what Jesus would do on the cross. He would give up his own life, hating it as it were. By doing that eternal life would be possible.

But Jesus made it clear that the principle of the cross did not apply to him alone but also to all who would believe on him (v. 26). The person who serves Christ will follow him. And he will be willing to follow him to the cross. Jesus went to the cross, and that is where his servant must go too. That person the Father will honor and claim as his own. What Jesus was willing to do himself he requires of those who follow him.

Committing Himself to His Death (12:27-36)

Turning then from the crisis that confronted the believer in the willingness to submit to death for Christ, Jesus expressed his own crisis (v. 27). John's Gospel does not record the agony of prayer by Jesus in the Garden of Gethsemane (see Mark 14:34-36). This passage reflects that same agony and compresses it into one public statement. The struggle of his own soul in the acceptance of his mission of death for others is exposed. The identification of the Savior with the struggle that any human undergoes in finding and accepting the will of God shows the reality of the incarnation. As it would be difficult for a believer to be willing to take up the cross with Christ so was it difficult for the Christ to accept his own death.

But in the same breath with which Jesus struggled to be freed from that for which he had come, he also expressed compliance with the will of God. His very purpose for coming into the world was to bring redemption to humankind (v. 27). That he would do no matter what the personal cost.

As he expressed the willingness to submit himself to the Father's purpose he also asked the Father to glorify his name (v. 28). By that he meant that praise should come to the Father through the act of the obedient Son. In response to that request came a voice from heaven saying, "I have glorified it, and I will glorify it again" (v. 28). Past and future are brought together. The Father had been glorified in the past by his true character being expressed by the acts of Jesus, and in the future his character and will would be made known through Christ to his praise. The Father confirmed the decision of the Son. What he had purposed to do would indeed bring praise to God. The Fourth Gospel does not give an account of the transfiguration at which a voice from heaven gave approval to the ministry of Jesus (see Mark 9:7). Again, this event seems to be reflected by the voice from heaven in another context. The Father approved the Son and confirmed his mission to the world.

The people, however, were not sure what to make of the sound. Apparently they heard the sound from heaven but were not able to understand it. Some interpreted it as a natural phenomenon, thunder. The voice of God had spoken, and they thought of it only as a natural occurrence, paying no more heed to it than to a peal of thunder. Others looked for a supernatural explanation, saying that an angel had spoken (v. 29).

Jesus gave a divine explanation to the voice from heaven (v. 30). It had not come on his account. He already knew that his acceptance of his mission was approved by the Father. The voice, instead, came to encourage and to inform them. Any of them who would hear and heed the voice would know that the act of Jesus in self-sacrifice was authenticated by the Father.

This led him to proclaim that the judgment of the world had now come (v. 31). By his death and resurrection the world would be judged by their acceptance or rejection of him. The one whom many considered the ruler of the world, Satan, would be defeated by this event. His power over human beings would be forever destroyed by Christ.

In contrast to Satan, whose power was destroyed by the cross, Jesus would be lifted up and exalted by the cross (v. 32). That was true literally as he was lifted up above the surface of the earth by the cross. But it was also true spiritually, since by the cross he was exalted. By being lifted up on the cross he would draw all persons to him. That did not mean that everyone would be saved; that would depend on one's personal faith. But it did indicate a universal salvation. Salvation was for anyone who would look to Christ in faith. Whereas the Jewish religion was exclusive, salvation through the crucified Christ is inclusive.

His reference to being lifted up was a cryptic reference to death by the cross (v. 33), a Roman method of execution. The people caught that reference. They quoted their understanding of the scriptural (Old Testament) teaching that the Messiah would rule forever. It was perhaps a reference to the promise of the permanence of a Davidic ruler (see 2 Sam. 7:12-13; Ps. 89:36). They still could not shake the concept of a nationalistic deliverer who would lead the nation to renewed strength. So they asked the question point-blank: "Who is this Son of man?" (v. 34). Understanding the Son of man as a messianic title, they could tell that their idea of the Son of man must conflict with Jesus' idea of the Son of man. To help clear up their understanding they put the question directly to him.

As he had done earlier, Jesus did not directly answer their

question (v. 35). Instead he urged them to follow the light that they had while there was still opportunity. He had already proclaimed himself "the light of the world" (8:12). And he had already informed them that he would not always be present and alive with them. They had enough light already to know that he was the Son of man who had been promised by the Father. What they needed to do then was to act on the light that they had rather than standing around discussing the fine points of their own conceptions. As a traveler walking in the late afternoon can be overtaken by nightfall, so they needed to act on the knowledge they already had while they had that opportunity. Many of them were living in darkness. Those who responded to the light by belief in Christ would become themselves children of the light (v. 36). They, too, would be characterized by light.

In summary fashion, Jesus presented the alternatives before them. Pointing out the urgency of decision, Jesus concluded his remarks to them and excused himself. By indicating that he hid himself from them, the Gospel writer does not mean that he hid out in fear somewhere, but rather that he no longer made himself available to them (v. 36). His public ministry was drawing to a close. Those who would come to the light, to life, would have to do so soon, for he would not be with them much longer.

Refusing to Believe Jesus (12:37-50)

His portrayal of Jesus' public ministry finished, the Gospel writer sought to explain why people had refused to believe Jesus. He had done many great signs before them, more than the seven recorded in this Gospel (v. 37). Yet, even in the face of these manifestations of God's power at work through Jesus, they had refused to believe on him. The explanation could be found in prophetic precedent. Quoting Isaiah 53:1 and 6:10, he showed that the people had simply fulfilled what their own Scriptures had predicted (vv. 38-40). This does not mean that God caused their unbelief. It is the use of the prophetic statement that presents a fact as though it had already happened. God was aware that they would not all believe, and the prophet stated it as an accomplished fact. The prophet pointed forward to the Christ. He anticipated his glory and warned of unbelief. But the people brought to pass what Isaiah had warned against (v. 41).

Not everyone rejected him, however. There were some of the Jewish authorities who believed him (v. 42). Tragically, they were afraid to express their faith openly since the Pharisees would put those who professed faith in Christ out of the synagogue and, thus, out of participation in worship. Jesus had sought the praise of God in his obedience to God. But some people were so anxious for the praise of men that they hid their faith in the Christ. The praise of the people they could see every day took precedence over the praise of God who was greater but whom they did not see daily (v. 43).

At some unspecified time Jesus summarized the theme of his teaching. Likely this is a summary statement given by the Gospel writer at this point as it closes the public ministry of Jesus. The one who believed Jesus believed the Father who sent him as the Father is seen through him (vv. 44-45). He came to give light to those who walked in the darkness (v. 46). While Jesus came to save the world rather than judge the world, judgment occurs in relation to what one does with Jesus Christ (vv. 47-48). One pronounces judgment upon oneself by the decision made about Christ. Jesus spoke with the authority of the Father and at the command of the Father (v. 49). The commandment that he communicated to persons was life itself (v. 50). What he had come to do in his ministry with persons he had done. He had expressed the commandment of the Father that new life is found by accepting Christ and walking in the light he had shed about God. He had brought a true and valid witness to God. What one does with that witness depends upon the individual's response to the Word God has spoken in revelation of himself.

Suffering

13:1 to 20:31

The public ministry of Jesus had drawn to a close. Through the signs and the discourses Jesus had revealed the Father to the old Israel as the one sent by the Father to redeem them. By faith Jesus had gathered a new Israel, a new people of God.

Beginning with chapter 13, Jesus emphasized his ministry to

these people of faith who had seen the light and walked in that light to life. With few exceptions, in chapters 13 to 20 his words are addressed to believers. No more signs are performed in public, and no more public discourses are recorded. The disciples, who occupied a minor part in the first part of the Gospel, take on a more significant role.

Whereas chapters 2 to 12 centered on his signs, chapters 13 to 20 center on his suffering. All the action takes place within one inclusive week: the week of his death. The place is Jerusalem. The event is his crucifixion, which he had predicted himself. That is followed by his resurrection from the dead. By the manner in which it is presented it is clear that the crucifixion did not occur because events got out of hand but as a part of God's redemptive purpose. And the presentation sweeps one to the conclusion that Jesus is indeed the Christ, God's promised one, through whom anyone who believes on Christ has life (20:31).

Training (13:1 to 17:26)

In a section often called the farewell discourses Jesus gave training to the twelve apostles for life on this earth without his physical presence. This section brings together a comprehensive presentation of his training; some of this is in the Synoptic Gospels. If it all occurred at one time, it probably was an extended discussion that began with the events of the Last Supper. Then it must have proceeded as Jesus and his disciples went from the upper room across the Temple precincts through the Kidron Valley to the slopes of Mount Olive to the Garden of Gethsemane where the arrest took place. To piece together that progression the material of the farewell discourses has to be overlaid on the accounts of the Synoptic Gospels. Others see it as a discourse delivered at the Passover meal where an address was usually delivered.

The Last Supper (13:1-38)

John's Gospel does not record the institution of the Lord's Supper, as do the Synoptic Gospels. There is the account of the observance of the Passover meal with Jesus and the disciples. This is generally considered the Last Supper at which the Lord's Supper was instituted, even though it is not specifically noted at what place in the meal that occurred.

Washing the disciple's feet (13:1-11).—Prior to the decisive Passover itself, Jesus had a meal with his disciples. He knew that the hour to which his life had pointed—the hour of his death by which he would be glorified—had arrived. As he had come into the world from the Father, he would depart from the world to the Father. He loved those who had come to him by faith to the utmost. He loved them as far as love could go—to the end (v. 1). He would soon show them his love by his death for them. Into his hands God had put all that would bring about this redemption. The cross was no accident. The entire life of Christ had pointed to that time (v. 3).

Not only did Jesus know that his hour had arrived, he also knew that Judas would betray him (v. 2). The satanic idea of the betrayal of Jesus had already been planted in the heart of Judas and received by him. The control that Jesus had over the whole event is again emphasized.

During the course of this meal Jesus got up from the table, took off his outer garments, wrapped a towel around his waist, poured water into a basin, and began to wash the feet of the disciples (vv. 4-5). Their feet extended to the ends of the couches on which they reclined on their left arms while eating. This washing was the work of a slave. It was usually done as a matter of courtesy upon arrival, rather than during a meal. That Jesus washed their feet during the meal made it more dramatic. And if it is correct, as the Synoptic Gospels seem to indicate, that the disciples were arguing among themselves as to who was greatest on the way to the meal (Luke 22:24-27), the drama is even heightened. They were not about to do the work of a slave. But the greatest of all would show that he was servant of all. He who would soon lay down his life for them had assumed the place of a servant.

As he got to Simon Peter, Peter asked Jesus in astonishment if he would wash his feet (v. 6). Without answering him directly, Jesus remarked that although Peter did not understand what Jesus was doing at the time he would understand it later (v. 7).

Characteristically, Peter protested that he would not let him wash his feet (v. 8). Jesus replied that if he did not wash him, he would have no part with Jesus. Cleansing by Christ is the only way one enters relationship with him. Again, Peter impulsively requested that if that were true Christ should not only wash his feet but also his hands and his head (v. 9). If washing some of his body were necessary, he was ready to go all the way. But Jesus corrected that impulsive comment also. It was like the person who had already bathed then walked a short distance. When he arrived at another house he would not require another bath, just the dust washed from his feet. They had already been cleansed by Christ (v. 10). But they needed to be reminded of the cost of that cleansing.

This was an enacted parable by Jesus. He who had been sent from God would be as obedient to the Father as a servant. Like a servant he would lay aside his own will to accept the will of the Father. By his death on the cross they would be cleansed from their sin. And it was Christ who had cleansed them completely. They had already made a commitment to him.

But there was one of them who had not made that complete commitment. Judas would betray him. Because of that Jesus could not make the blanket statement that all were clean (v. 11).

Observing the Last Supper (13:12-35).—Completing the task of washing the disciples' feet, Jesus put on his outer garments and took his place at the table. Then he asked them if they understood what he had just done (v. 12). Without waiting for them to give an answer, he observed that they called him both Teacher and Lord. And that was right. He taught them the truths of God, and he was the Lord of their lives (v. 13). But if he as their Teacher and Lord would stoop to the place of humble service to wash their feet, they also ought to wash one another's feet (v. 14). He had given them an example to follow. Whether literally washing the feet of another or not, any believer in Christ must follow his example in the willingness to perform lowly, humble, thankless service to others.

In the manner of a solemn pronouncement he reminded them that the servant is not greater than the master (v. 16). What he did they should do. Neither is the one sent greater than the one who sent him. He was sending them out into the world to bear witness of the Christ, and they were to perform a similar kind of self-sacrificing service in his name. In the form of a beatitude (v. 17) he indicated that they were blessed if they both knew and did those things. It is one thing to know such lofty spiritual principles; it is quite another thing to put them into practice. But, for it to be effective, knowledge must be translated into practice.

The treachery of Judas obviously weighed heavily upon Jesus' mind. Once more he indicated that he was not talking about all of them, for one of them would betray him (v. 18). He had, however, chosen all of them, even the betrayer. The betrayer's actions would only bear out a scriptural passage found in Psalm 41:9. It was an unnatural act, rather like the modern proverb about a dog that bites the hand that feeds him. One chosen by the Savior would be expected to follow the Savior in faith. But Judas had sold out completely to evil. Jesus was telling them this beforehand so that they would not be too surprised when it happened (v. 19). They would know by the events that he was truly the one from God.

Jesus would send them out in his name, by his authority. With the solemn and noteworthy pronouncement he showed that those who received—that is, believed and accepted the witness—the ones he sent would receive him. And the one who received Jesus would receive the Father who had sent him. There is a progression of reception by faith that leads directly to the Father. By accepting his mission they were accepting him.

Although Jesus had indicated earlier that one of them would betray him (6:70; 13:10,18) the disciples apparently had not taken it seriously. But Jesus took it seriously, so seriously that at the meal he was agitated by it. He stated it to them plainly and seriously, "Truly, truly, I say to you, one of you will betray me" (v. 21). It could hardly have been put more directly or solemnly than that.

This time it caught their attention. Interestingly enough, none of them seemed so sure of his own commitment that he did not question himself. Looking around the group each one wondered who it was and had to question whether it was himself (see Mark 14:19). Simon Peter signaled to a disciple identified only as one of the disciples whom Jesus loved (v. 23) to find out from Jesus the identity of the betrayer (v. 24). The seating arrangement at the table seemed to position Judas at the left and the beloved disciple at the right of Jesus. The diners reclined on their left arm on a couch with the right arm and hand free to get food. The disciple who would be lying close to the breast of Jesus would be the one to his right, perhaps even sharing the same couch. It would be easy enough for him to lean toward Jesus and whisper the question to him. The answer could be given without everyone at the table hearing it. The disciple whom Jesus loved is not identified, though it traditionally has been thought to be John. Some, however, have thought it may have been Lazarus who was not one of the twelve. The reader of the Gospel of John knows the identity of the betrayer, but the disciples did not.

Jesus answered the question by saying that it was the one to whom he would give a piece of food, bread or meat, dipped in the sauce or gravy. This was considered an act of friendship or honor (v. 26). Apparently as he dipped the food into the sauce, possibly while still speaking in a hushed tone, he gave it to Judas and also gave him an instruction, "What you are going to do, do quickly" (v. 27).

Those at the table did not understand the impact of the statement. Apparently the beloved disciple did not understand it either or surely he would have attempted to stop Judas. They may not have understood it because they did not hear the quiet conversation. The disciple whom Jesus loved may not have understood it because Jesus possibly gave the food to Judas while still speaking. The disciples put two interpretations on the words of Jesus to Judas. One was that Judas was to buy the supplies they would need for the Passover celebration. Since he was the treasurer of the group he was also likely the purchasing agent. The other interpretation was that Jesus was dispatching him to make a customary gift to the poor from their common purse (v. 29).

When did Judas make his final decision to do his terrible deed? It could have been that he held the morsel of food a moment after receiving it from Jesus. Then the temptation of Satan was too much for him, and his decision was recalled (v. 27). Judas cannot be excused from his action by saying that he was possessed by Satan. The temptation may have come from Satan, but the decision was made by Judas. Neither can Judas' action be explained by surmising that he really did not mean to betray Jesus, that he was only trying to force him into a decisive action that would show him to be the Messiah. The personal responsibility for Judas' actions, as for all human actions, rests on the person himself. Judas made the decision. Jesus had given him every opportunity to reconsider. On more than one occasion he had let it be known that he knew a betrayer was with them. Even his act of giving the food to Judas was a last appeal of love. But Judas rebuffed this expression of love and left the table.

When Judas left the group it was night (v. 30). This is more than a notation of the time of day. It was also an expression of the darkness of the deed. Jesus had come to lead persons into light. But one of those closest to him had chosen to reject the light of the world and to walk in darkness. Into the darkness of the night he went to carry out his dark, dastardly deed.

When Judas left the apostolic group the final decision leading to Jesus' destiny had been reached. Jesus had indicated many times earlier that his "hour" would come when he would be glorified. With the departure of Judas he could say, "Now is the Son of man glorified" (v. 31). The time had arrived for his glorification.

But it was a mutual glorification between the Father and the Son. As Jesus would be glorified by the event of the crucifixion and the resurrection, so would the Father be glorified by it. Glorification means that the true and full character can be known for the praise of God. Both the Father and the Son would be shown for what they were through the death of Jesus upon the cross and his resurrection from the dead (v. 32). His obedience to the Father would magnify and exalt both of them.

Speaking affectionately to the disciples by calling them little children, Jesus informed them that he would be with them personally and physically only a little while longer (v. 33). He would no longer be physically with them, and they would try to find him. He had told the Jews earlier the same thing (8:21), that they could not go where he was going.

Then he gave to them a new commandment of love (v. 34). It was fitting that his first words in the farewell discourse had to do with love since love was the interpretation of his death and resurrection. The commandment to the followers of Jesus Christ is to love one another. The measure of that love is also spelled out—as he loved. No follower of Jesus need ever wonder how much to love. Jesus expressed it by the extent of his love—obedience, even to the death.

Jesus called this a new commandment. It was not entirely new, as Jesus had mentioned love before. Jesus breathed new life into an old commandment. How is this a new commandment? T. B. Maston in *Biblical Ethics* points out that, as Jesus presented this commandment to love, it was new in its source: "I give to you"; in its motive: "as I have loved you"; in its nature: an obedience growing out of a new relationship; and in its dimensions: a distinctive love for those in the Christian family.

A distinctive mark of the disciple of Christ was his love (v. 35). The way that people would know that they were his followers would be through the quality of their love for one another. To follow Jesus in that kind of love was not to embark on an uncharted course. He had showed them how to love in his humble service of washing their feet (vv. 1-11), and he would also show them in his sacrificial death on the cross.

The farewell discourse proper began with this discussion following the departure of Judas. When he left the end was in sight. And Jesus began to share with them those important matters he wanted them to know.

Predicting Peter's denial (13:36-38).—The farewell discourse moves forward on the questions that are asked Jesus and his answers and amplifications to those questions. Simon Peter started it off with the first question.

Peter wanted to know where Jesus was going (v. 36). As he had already said, Jesus reminded him that he could not go where he was going at that time. But then he said that Peter would go there later. This could have reference to going to the presence of the Father. Jesus would ascend to the Father following the resurrection. Peter would not go there then but would later join him there (14:1-3). Or it could have reference to the suffering that they would share with him. Jesus was going to his death. Those who followed him in faith, including Simon Peter, would also follow him in suffering for that faith.

Apparently picking up on the latter meaning, Peter vowed that he would be willing to lay down his life for Jesus (v. 37). He really did not understand why he could not go with him then. He would be willing to follow him even to death, using the same terms that Jesus had used for his death.

Would he really follow him all the way, even to death? Jesus questioned it, knowing that Peter had spoken hastily. Then he predicted that even before morning Peter would deny him three times (v. 38). The loyalty of which he had boasted would not last even till morning. All of the Gospels record this prediction of Peter's denial. Obedient faith is not easy to come by. Jesus solemnly noted this.

The Way to the Father (14:1-31)

Discussion with Thomas (14:1-7).—The disciples of Jesus had reason for troubled hearts. Jesus had told them that he was going away (13:33), that one of them would betray him (13:21), and that one of them would deny him three times before morning (13:38). To calm their troubled hearts Jesus told them to believe in God. And since they believed in God they would also believe in him. By the same token, by believing in him they believed in God (v. 1). The identity of Jesus and the Father was so complete that belief in one demanded belief in the other.

Still answering Peter's question about where he was going (13:36), Jesus promised that he was going to the Father's house to prepare a place for them (v. 2). The implication is that if he was going there and if he was preparing a place for them he was also expecting them to show up there. The Father's house had many rooms or abiding places. There would be room enough and to spare for all to have an abiding place in the Father's house. The reference to the Father's house may have been suggested by the prominence of the Temple, which was often called the Father's house (2:16), in their thoughts that week. Or it could have had a reference to the upper room where they were perhaps even then still gathered. As he had sent two of the disciples on ahead earlier to prepare the upper room (Mark 14:12-16) for them, so Jesus would go ahead of the disciples to prepare an eternal dwelling place in the Father's house for them.

This is a promise with two dimensions. On the one hand, it is a future promise that the believer will live in the roominess of the Father's house with perfect fellowship forever. On the other hand, it is a present promise that Jesus calms the troubled heart with the assurance that he has prepared both the place and the way and will always be present with his believers to strengthen and guide them. Both in the hope of heaven and the help on earth the Savior can be trusted to have prepared the way.

The truth of Jesus' preparation is pledged by his own trustworthiness. He would not have promised that he would prepare a place for his followers if that was not true. Jesus never gave a promise that he could not fulfill.

In addition to that, having prepared a place for the believer he would return to take the believer with him. The result will be a shared relationship for all eternity (v. 3). He had already told them where he was going by previously mentioning that he would return to the Father who had sent him. And he had already shown them the way by his teachings (v. 4).

But Thomas wanted it spelled out more specifically (v. 5). He wanted to be able to know without doubt both the destination of the Savior and the way to it.

In another of his claims Jesus centered the answer to the question in himself (v. 6). He was the way to the Father. It was not just that he showed the way to the Father by revealing it; he was the way to the Father by redeeming persons. He was also the truth. Divine reality rested in him. He was totally reliable to express the truth of God and his salvation. And he was the life. He was both the source and the content of life. To know Jesus is to have life. The destination to the Father and ultimately to the Father's house is personal. It is centered in the person of Jesus Christ. And it is relational. It is based on a personal relationship by faith to Jesus Christ. It is also exclusive. Only through Jesus Christ can one come to the Father. To know Jesus Christ in the personal relationship of faith is to have access to the Father and thus to the Father's house.

To know Jesus is to know the Father (v. 7). Jesus came to earth to reveal God and to redeem humankind. In accepting Jesus Christ by faith any person both knows and sees the Father. The way to the Father is through the Son.

Discussion with Philip (14:8-14).—The statement concerning the unity of the Father and the Son in Jesus Christ prompted Philip to ask to see the Father. He would be satisfied if he could just see the Father (v. 8). He had heard enough of explanations and interpretations; to lay eyes on the Father would remove all their difficulties.

It must have been with some difficulty that Jesus kept himself from showing impatience with Philip when he asked him if he had been with them so long and he still did not know him (v. 9). The person who had seen Jesus had seen all that human eyes could see of the Father. Jesus had come to the earth to declare the Father to human beings (1:18). It seemed hard to comprehend that Philip still had to ask to see the Father after he had seen Jesus.

Did he not believe in the mutual identity of Father and Son

(v. 10)? In believing in Jesus he would have believed in the Father. In seeing Jesus he would have seen the Father. The very words that Jesus had spoken had come from the Father. He did not speak by his own authority but by the power of the Father. Neither did he do the works that he had done in his own power. It was by the power of the Father that Jesus was able to do the works that had attracted such attention to him.

It came down to a matter of faith. He was to believe Jesus in the unity of the Father and the Son, that he was in the Father and the Father was in him (v. 11). He had said it; they should believe it. Or, if that were too hard, they should have believed him because of the works he did. Remember that the writer of John's Gospel called the miracles *signs*; they were signs that pointed beyond themselves to God. Remember, also, that Jesus called these miracles *works*. What was to human minds a miracle was simply a work to Jesus. All these things were done by God's power. Throughout the Gospel of John the belief induced by a miracle was not considered the highest level of belief (2:23-25, for instance); but it was belief. Better to believe Jesus on the basis of a sign that pointed to God than not to believe him at all.

The belief in the complete communion and the total unity between Father and Son was applied in two areas. In the first of these areas of application, Jesus promised in solemn pronouncement that the person believing in him would do greater works that even he did (v. 12). The reason for this possibility is that Jesus would go to the Father. He would no longer be present on the earth to act in power. While it is only hinted here and made explicit later, as Jesus went to the Father the Holy Spirit would come to infill and to empower the life of the believer. Jesus was present on the earth for a very limited time. The believers would be present for a longer span of time. That promise was carried out on the Day of Pentecost, as one illustration, when on one day more believers were added to Christ than throughout his whole life (Acts 2:41).

The second area of application given by Jesus was in prayer. The promise of power in prayer is promised (v. 13). The scope of prayer is unlimited. Anything that is asked in his name will be given. "In his name" is not simply a formula for prayer or a structure for prayer. What is asked in his name must be consistent with his name, that is, consistent with his character. To ask something in the name of Christ is to request matters that conform to rather than contradict the character and the concepts of the Christ. These requests will be answered in order that the Father might be glorified through the Son. They would see that the Father and Son are one when those requests offered in conformity with the character of the Son are done through the power of the Father. As what he did on earth glorified the Father, so would answered prayer bring glory and praise to the Father. This was his promise to his followers (v. 14).

Discussion with Judas (14:15-24).—The promise of Jesus to answer prayer offered in his name is not unconditional. The condition is love. The prayer offered in the name of Jesus and the life-style of the follower of Jesus are marked by love. The one who loves Jesus will live a life of obedience to him (v. 15).

Jesus gave to his disciples the first of several promises of the presence of the Holy Spirit (v. 16; see also v. 26; 15:26; 16:7). The Holy Spirit is identified as the Counselor. This is a legal term also translated the Advocate or the Comforter or sometimes not actually translated and called the Paraclete. It means one called to stand alongside another. And since Jesus indicated that the Holy Spirit was "another" Counselor it meant another of the same kind; the Holy Spirit would not be different from Jesus himself. Since Jesus would pray that the Father would send the Counselor to them it is regarded as a gift of God. Whereas Jesus would soon be absent from them the Holy Spirit would always be present with them.

A second name given to the Holy Spirit by Jesus was "the Spirit of truth" (v. 17). He would be the Spirit that communicated truth. Jesus had identified himself as truth (v. 6), and those who worship the Father must do so in truth (4:23). The truth that is God and that is God's word to humankind is made known through the Holy Spirit.

The world at large, the world without God, could not know that Spirit of truth. That is not surprising since they had not recognized the truth in Jesus. Because the world has not received him it could neither see nor know the Spirit of truth. But the believers could know because through Jesus Christ the Spirit of truth both lived with them and lived in them.

In Old Testament times, the presence of the Holy Spirit was occasional and special. The Spirit of God came upon persons to do a special act for God. The promise of Jesus was that the Holy Spirit would be personal and permanent. He would be given to those who believed in Jesus and would reside in their hearts. Jesus would not always be physically present with those who followed him, but the Holy Spirit would.

Jesus assured them that he would not leave them desolate, actually as orphans (v. 18). He would come again to them. This is the second reference (v. 3) to a return of the Lord to them. This has often been understood as a reference to the second coming of Christ. Others have interpreted it as the immediate return to them in the appearances after the resurrection. Or it could be a continued reference to the Counselor who would give them strength and guidance. While all three possibilities are in the background to the statement, probably the last is the clearest meaning at this point.

It would only be a little while that the world could see him. Then it would see him no more, but his followers would (v. 19). At that time they would be aware of the threefold relationship of unity between the Father, the Son, and the believer (v. 20). This unity is based on the love that allows one to keep the commandments of Christ. The one who follows Jesus in obedient love is loved by the Father and the Son. And the Christ will be manifested to him (v. 21). The believers will also share in the kind of relationship enjoyed by Jesus and the Father. It would take his death on the cross, resurrection from the dead, and the gift of the Holy Spirit before they would realize the meaning of all this.

The mention of manifestation brought the question from Judas of a physical, visible, spectacular manifestation of the Christ (v. 22). Even after all that time and all that talk the disciples had trouble separating their belief in Jesus from the traditional concepts of the Messiah. Judas—and the Gospel writer is clear to point out that this was not Judas Iscariot, who had already left the group (13:30)—wanted to know how this manifestation could be to them and not to the world. If it were the kind of manifestation they had always imagined the world would know, too.

Jesus again made the point that the true manifestation is through love (vv. 23-24). The manifestation of which he spoke then was not physical but spiritual. It has an ethical dimension in that the way a person loves and follows Christ in obedient love shows how he has received the manifestation of the Messiah. The one who loves him will be obedient to him. The one who does not love him will not be obedient to him. The things that he has spoken were from the

Father. The Father and the Son will have a home in the heart of the person who responds to Jesus in love.

Discussion with the disciples (14:25-31).—Jesus explained to the disciples that he had spoken these words of encouragement and strength to them while he was still present with them (v. 25). This close to his death one could expect words of doom and despair. Instead, they are words of encouragement, hope, and victory.

He reminded them that the Counselor would be sent by the Father in his name (v. 26). The unity of action of the Father and the Son are apparent as the Counselor, called at this place the Holy Spirit comes from both the Father and the Son. One of the things the Holy Spirit will do is to continue the teachings of Jesus. He would prompt their memories to bring to mind what Jesus had taught. And there will also be a unity in these teachings. The things taught by the Holy Spirit will conform to rather than contradict the teachings of Jesus.

A portion of the legacy of love left to his followers by Jesus is peace (v. 27). The peace given by Jesus is contrasted with the peace of the world. The world's concept of peace is negative—the absence of war or strife. Christ's concept of peace is positive—peace in the midst of strife, even an impending execution by the cross. Their hearts can be calm and fearless in this time, and any time of stress, because of the distinctive peace given by the Prince of peace.

By telling them that he would go away from them, Jesus told them they should have joy rather than sorrow (v. 28). By his going away to come to them again he would go to the Father. Christ's self-limitation by the incarnation meant that the Father was greater than the Son. His going away would allow them to know a fullness of the power of God in their own lives.

He would not have much opportunity to talk further with them (vv. 29-30). He was preparing them for the time when he would go away so they would not be surprised when it happened. The forces of evil, expressed as the ruler of the world, would assert themselves and apparently win over him. But actually the ruler of the world had no power over Christ. The power of Satan must never be considered equal to or greater than the power of God. What Jesus did in laying down his life was voluntarily done. And this was done in loving obedience to the will of the Father (v. 31). Satan had no power over Jesus at the cross, and his power was totally and permanently broken by the resurrection. The cross did not happen because matters slipped out of the control of God.

By his command to "Rise, let us go hence" (v. 31) Jesus let them know that the time for talk was drawing to a close. Apparently they left the upper room and moved out toward the Garden of Gethsemane. The farewell discourse would continue as they made their way from Mount Zion, across the Temple area, through the Kidron Valley, and up the slopes of the Mount of Olives to the Garden of Gethsemane.

The True Vine (15:1-27)

As they left the upper room and crossed the Temple area to reach the Kidron Valley and the Mount of Olives they passed the Temple itself. On the front of the Temple was an elaborately embossed golden vine. Perhaps as they walked by the Temple and saw the familiar golden vine Jesus said to them, "I am the true vine" (v. 1).

They would have been familiar with the vine as a symbol of Israel in the Old Testament (Ps. 80:8; Isa. 5:1-7; Jer. 2:21, for example). During the period of independence under the Maccabees the vine was the symbol of the nation used on the coins. But in each of the Old Testament references to Israel as the vine the emphasis is on the degeneracy of the vine. With the symbol of the vine in the background of their thinking and the vine on the Temple before their eyes, Jesus stated that he was the true vine, the real and authentic vine. The nation Israel, symbolized by the vine, had grown wild, but Jesus had been obedient to the will of the Father. The Father was the gardener who tended and cared for the vine.

The gardener of the vine was so careful that he pruned the branches to encourage them to bear more fruit and cut off the unproductive branches (v. 2). He was not the kind of vinedresser who simply let his vines grow their own wild and undisciplined way. Instead, he exerted constant and concerned care over the vine so that it would be the most productive vine possible.

Then Jesus made the application of his metaphor fit his disciples. Referring to his previous comments to them (13:10), he indicated that they had been made clean through his word (v. 3). As the branches of a vine draw strength and sustenance from the vine, so were they strengthened and sustained by abiding in him (v. 4). By abiding in him they would be productive and fruitful. But the only way they could be fruitful was through abiding in him. The relationship of unity between the believer and Christ is as close as that of the branches and the vine. In fact, Jesus made it more explicit when he said, "I am the vine, you are the branches" (v. 5). A branch could not live unless it had a life-sustaining relationship to the vine. In this application Jesus made it clear that the believer lived in that kind of life-sustaining union with himself. Without that union they could do nothing. In that union they could be productive.

The fruit for the Christian is a Christlike life. It is the reproduction of those characteristics of life expressed in Jesus Christ himself. As he lived in love and followed the Father's will in obedience the believer is to be marked by those same traits.

There is a pruning process that goes on (v. 6). With the cultivation of any vine the dead wood is cut off and the branches are cut back so they can produce more. Judas Iscariot had already left the group. At one point, many turned back from following him (6:66). Others whose commitment was only lip service would also leave. True disciples would remain faithful to the end. The disciplining of the disciples would go on. They would face hard times and tough decisions during the arrest, trial, and crucifixion. Yet through the discipline of pruning a hardier, more productive vine results. The abiding relationship with the vine is essential for life.

One of the promises of the abiding relationship is answered prayer (v. 7). Notice that the relationship with Christ is not simply emotional and subjective. As the believer abides in Christ and the words of Christ abide in him, the believer can ask in prayer and receive the answer. It is not a matter of any whim being granted but of maintaining such a relationship to Christ in faith and in conformity with his teachings that what one asks would be in line with God's will. The Father is glorified through the answered prayer (v. 8). The things they ask and what they want would be in such conformity with the character of Christ and the will of God that the result would bring glory and praise to God. The proof of the disciple is a character in conformity with the character of Christ.

The Father had loved the Son. Jesus' whole life with the disciples had been spent in the love of the Father. And he loved them (v. 9). They, too, were to live in his love. Disciples of Christ can live in the knowledge of his love; they also can live in the strength of his love.

And having experienced the love of Christ they are to express the love of Christ.

Obedience is a mark of discipleship (v. 10). Jesus lived his life in loving obedience to the commandment of the Father. The believer is to live his life in loving obedience to Christ. Abiding in his love is to obey his will and to live his way of life.

Joy is a result of discipleship (v. 11). The late Sam Shoemaker once observed that joy is the surest mark of a Christian. As Christians abide in Christ the joy of Christ fills their lives. Believers experience the fullness of joy as it comes through Christ. Remember that these words were spoken just before an arrest, a trial, and an execution. They were spoken to a group of people whose hearts were troubled while Jesus was staring death in the face. Jesus prepared them for life and witness on the earth without his physical presence. And joy was one of the results of a living, sustaining relationship with him even in those circumstances.

He repeated his great commandment to them: to love one another. He had given it to them already as a new commandment (13:34) and now he repeated it for emphasis as it followed on the heels of his telling them to live in his love. If they lived in his love it would express itself by love for one another. One cannot love the Father without loving the siblings also. The measure of that love is also expressed: as he has loved them. How much did he love them? To the extent of laying down his life for them. And this is to be the measure of the love of Christians for one another. There is no greater expression of love for another than to give one's life for the other (v. 13). Jesus expressed the greatness of his love by that act and challenged those who follow him to do the same. William Barclay once said that Christians sometime live as though they were sent into the world to compete, dispute, or quarrel with one another, when really they were sent into the world to live in such a way as to show what it means to love one another.

Having observed that the greatest expression of love is the laying down of a life for a friend, Jesus said that friendship with him came with obedience to him (v. 14). He would call them his friends from that time on. He would no longer call them servants, literally slaves (v. 15). The reason for that switch in relationship was that a servant did not know, nor did he have to know, what his master did or why he did it. Unquestioned obedience was demanded. But Jesus was calling them friends because he had shared with them all that he had received from the Father. He was letting them in on what was happening, why it was happening, and what their continued relationship with him would be in the light of it. This is true friendship. As his friends they would have access to him and live in intimacy with him.

It was a friendship that he had initiated. He had chosen them (v. 16). And as he had chosen them he had also commissioned them. They were commissioned to go out into the world and to win others to the same kind of abiding relationship with him. This was not a circle of friendship that excluded other people. It was a circle of friendship that included others. It was an ever-increasing circle of folk who were reached for Christ. The productiveness of the Christlike life results in other persons becoming Christians. And all Christians exist in a relationship to Christ of such unity that it is described as a vine and its branches. The promise of answered prayer is a part of this. Once again they were reminded to love one another (v. 17). To have been repeated so often this must have been a real concern for Jesus. He was so interested in his followers loving one another that three times in the farewell discourse he gave it as a commandment (13:34; vv. 12,17).

As the disciples share the privilege of being included in the love of the Father so do they share the problem of being involved in the world's hatred and rejection of Jesus (v. 18). This should come as no surprise to them. Since the world hated and rejected Jesus it would also hate and reject his followers who had been commissioned to reproduce his character in the world. The "world" does not refer to the created world. It refers to the world of people without God and opposed to God.

The world has always had problems with those things and persons different from it. Difference normally begets doubt. And this leads to dispute and rejection. Jesus had chosen them out of the world (v. 19). This would indicate both that he had chosen them from out of the world's population and also that he had chosen them to be different from the world's expectation. To be chosen by Christ is to be a different kind of person. And the world always has trouble dealing with that. This truth is backed up by a proverbial saying that the servant is never greater than his master (v. 20) which he had already shared with them (13:16). Since the world at large had persecuted Christ they could expect persecution as his followers. If the world at large had received his message it would receive theirs also. But it had not.

The reason the world had not received his message was that it had not received the Father who sent him (v. 21). In failing to know the Father by faith and through experience they had rejected the Son. And in rejecting the Son they would also reject those who followed the Son in faith.

By the coming of Christ to the world the sin of the world is increased (v. 22). They could not be held responsible for the sin of rejecting the Father if they had never heard the truth about the Father. But through Jesus' coming into the world and in his making God known the guilt of those who reject the Father is increased. They know what they are rejecting. As those who loved and received Jesus both knew and received the Father, so those who hated and rejected Jesus both hated and rejected God (v. 23). The unity between the Father and the Son works in both directions. By bringing his message to them and working his works of grace among them they had personal responsibility for their rejection of God (v. 24). They were rejecting a clear witness to God. In the Psalms (35:19; 69:4) there is reference to hating him without a cause. Ironically, those who were supposed to have known the Scriptures best were guilty of living out that statement because they had hated and rejected both the Father and the Son.

In that atmosphere of persecution, hatred, and rejection the disciples would live following the departure of Jesus from the earth. It was the same atmosphere in which he had lived. They would but share his own reception by the world apart from God. And into that atmosphere the Counselor would come for their help and strength. The Counselor would be sent by the Son and would come from the Father (v. 26). The interaction between the Father, the Son, and the Holy Spirit shows the unity between them. As Trinitarian Christians, the disciples were reminded that Father, Son, and Holy Spirit are one while they are experienced separately. The Trinity is a doctrine of experience.

By calling the Holy Spirit the Spirit of truth, the author of John's Gospel emphasized witness as a work of the Holy Spirit. The Holy Spirit gives witness to the truth of Jesus' witness of God. The witness that the Holy Spirit will give and the leadership of the Holy

Spirit in a life will never be contrary to the life and teachings of Jesus Christ. The Spirit of truth bears witness to the truth that Jesus has shown.

Another supporting witness is that of the disciples (v. 27). A dual witness to the truth of Jesus Christ comes from the disciples and the Holy Spirit. Those who have experienced faith in Jesus Christ give testimony to the life-changing character of that faith. That witness is backed up by the witness of the Holy Spirit. The Holy Spirit leads persons to faith through the witness of believers in Christ.

The witness of the first disciples had additional weight due to the fact that they had been with Jesus from the beginning. What he had said and what he had done could be verified by their witness. The world is not left without its witness of Christ. Thus in rejecting Christ and the Father who sent him the world bears its own burden of guilt.

The Gift of the Spirit (16:1-33)

Jesus continued his preparation of the disciples for the pattern of persecution they would endure. These matters were being revealed to them so they would have strength when they occurred (v. 1). Warning them against expulsion from the synagogue and threats against their lives (v. 2), Jesus indicated that the persecution would shift from him to them. While he was with them the religious authorities took out their feelings and frustrations against him. But after his departure they would turn on the disciples. There was ample reason to issue both these warnings as they had expelled the man who had been healed of his blindness from the synagogue (9:34) and had plotted to kill Lazarus after he had been raised from the dead (12:10). The type of persecution envisioned at this time was not an official policy of governmental persecution as much as the persecution by those self-righteous persons who felt they were serving God by opposing Jesus and his followers.

The reason for their actions against Jesus and his followers was ignorance. It was not an intellectual ignorance in that they did not know but a moral and spiritual ignorance in that they would not see (v. 3). Having refused Jesus and his witness to God they had also refused the Father. The disciple's "hour" of persecution and suffering would come as Jesus' "hour" of glorification was fast approaching. When the time came that they would suffer they would have been prepared for it. To be forewarned was to be forearmed. The fact of suffering for Jesus should not take his follower by surprise.

The main line of defense the disciples would have in the time of persecution would be the power of the Holy Spirit in their lives. Jesus detailed this resource for them. As long as he was physically present with them this resource was not necessary. He was there to strengthen, comfort, and guide. But with his departure the presence of the Holy Spirit was necessary.

Interestingly enough, even though he had spoken frequently of going away from them they had not sought to learn his destination (v. 5). At first this statement sounds unusual remembering Peter's question of 13:36. But that was a casual question that was not pursued. Their concern for themselves because Jesus was going away had overshadowed their concern for him and his ultimate destination (v. 6).

It was to the advantage of his believers that Jesus go away (v. 7). As long as he was physically present in the world he was limited to one place and to one group of persons, but with his departure and the presence of the Holy Spirit such limitations of place and people would be removed. The Holy Spirit performs his ministry at many places and with many persons simultaneously. In his going away he would send the Holy Spirit to them.

The ministry of the Holy Spirit to the world was outlined. In previous references to the Counselor or the Holy Spirit his ministry to the believers was emphasized, and the aspect of this ministry presented was defense. He would help to defend them. He would be actively present in their defense against the world. But at this time the role switched and the Holy Spirit was presented as the prosecutor (v. 8). The Holy Spirit functions as the prosecutor who secures the guilty verdict for the world which has rejected Christ. The prosecution is on three counts particularly: sin, righteousness, and judgment.

The conviction of sin is based on the fact that they had not believed Jesus (v. 9). The basic sin is the rejection of both the message and the messenger from God. Rejecting Jesus, they have opened themselves up to other expressions of self-will and rebellion.

The conviction of righteousness is based on the vindication of Jesus as Savior as he returned to the Father who had sent him (v. 10). They were convinced that right standing with God resulted from the keeping of the Law. They even considered themselves as having been pronounced right before God because they had kept the Law to the extent that they eliminated Jesus. But how wrong they were. Jesus went to be with the Father. They could not see him any longer. But his resurrection and ascension proved the cross to be the expression of the rightness of God, God's absolute standard of right, and the means of right standing with God.

The conviction of judgment came about through God's judgment on Satan by the cross (v. 11). Satan had been dubbed the ruler of the world. But God was shown without doubt to be the ruler of the world when the power of Satan was destroyed by the cross. Absolute judgment had been pronounced upon Satan. The condemnation of the tactics of the world of self-will and rebellion as expressed by Satan was complete.

Notice that all the areas of conviction of the world by the Holy Spirit center in Christ Jesus. By his death on the cross Jesus showed the real meaning of sin, righteousness, and judgment. By his death on the cross Jesus pronounced the verdict on the world in these three ways, and the Holy Spirit prosecutes the case until the verdict is returned.

Turning from the work of the Holy Spirit in the world Jesus informed them of the work of the Holy Spirit with the believer. At that point they could neither bear to hear nor interpret correctly all the things Jesus had to share with them (v. 12). But with the coming of the Holy Spirit, again referred to as the Spirit of truth, he would guide them into all truth (v. 13). The truth into which he would guide them was the truth revealed and expressed by Jesus. Any witness of the Holy Spirit is consistent with the truth that Jesus has made known. The leadership of the Holy Spirit will never be away from Jesus but to Jesus. What the Holy Spirit teaches is what Jesus has taught. The authority of the Holy Spirit is wrapped up in the authority of Jesus and the Father. There is a spiritual consistency between all three persons or expressions of the Godhead that will not be violated. The things to come that the Holy Spirit makes known are not detailed prophecies of future events so much as the understanding of what Jesus taught, the Christian faith.

The Holy Spirit will glorify Jesus (v. 14). Called by B. H. Carroll the "other Jesus," the Holy Spirit works to make Jesus known fully and thus to bring both glory and praise to him. The Holy Spirit emphasizes Jesus and not himself. The Holy Spirit will make known to believers what Jesus had received from the Father (v. 15). There is a direct relationship and an utter consistency between the work and the words of the Father, the Son, and the Holy Spirit. There is no pitting of one against the other. They each do the work of all. The Holy Spirit guides in making the truth of God as made known in Jesus Christ understood and applied in every age.

The disciples were confused by his statements concerning his going away and the time references to a little while (v. 16). They could not understand the indefinite time frame. And they were puzzled about the indications of going away and coming again. It is not always clear whether Jesus made reference in these statements to his coming again in the second coming, to the appearances after the resurrection, or to the presence of the Holy Spirit. Since the writer of John's Gospel made creative use of ambiguity there may have been an intentional device of allowing some latitude in the understanding of the references. Here, however, it seems to refer more to their seeing him after the resurrection since Jesus had made a distinction between the Holy Spirit and himself and since the promise of seeing him again seems more immediate.

Apparently they never framed the question that was bothering them. Jesus knew what they were thinking and answered it for them (v. 19). In supplying the answer he used the illustration of a woman giving birth to a child. During travail there is pain. But at the birth of the child joy is experienced. The pain becomes secondary. The primary emotion is joy. Their experience would be this paradoxical mixture of pain and sorrow (vv. 20-21). He had told them of the persecution and pain they would have to bear. His departure from them would bring sorrow to them; indeed, it was even then causing sorrow and confusion. But when they saw him again they would have overwhelming joy (v. 22). Others might have taken him away from them through his execution on the cross, but the joy resulting from his resurrection could not be taken from them (v. 22).

They had been asking him a lot of questions during the farewell discourse. And they had some other questions in mind that they did not voice. But then they would not ask him any questions. What he had been telling them would be clarified. They would have an understanding after the cross and the resurrection of what he had taught them concerning his going away and his coming again. They would also understand the meaning of the joy he had mentioned.

From the asking of questions Jesus turned to a different kind of asking: the asking in prayer (v. 23). They could have confidence in prayer in that anything they asked of the Father in his name they would receive. By asking in his name the assumption is made that what they asked would be consistent with his character and his teachings. Before Jesus came they had made requests of the Father. But now they would ask the Father in the name of the Son, in his authority and in accordance with his will. And they would be answered. This would bring joy to them. They could know the joy of which Jesus had spoken because of the assurances of prayer (v. 24).

Up to this time Jesus had spoken to them in figures of speech and in parables. He had used the imagery of the woman in travail (v. 21) and the vine and the branches (15:1), for instance. He used these to convey to them his message so they could understand and apply it to their immediate situation. But the time would come when he could speak plainly to them (v. 25). He would tell them of the Father. He would assure them of answered prayer from the Father (v. 26). He would emphasize the unity of the Father and the Son. What he had done he had done in the power of the Father. What he had taught he had taught on the authority of the Father. The Father loved them because they have loved Jesus and believed him. Through belief in Jesus they have also believed the Father. Jesus had come into the world from the Father. But he would also leave the world and return to the Father (v. 28). It has been observed that this one verse (v. 28) contains the preexistence of Christ, his incarnation, his death, and his ascension in four short phrases. He had very plainly told them once again of what he had done in the world and what would happen to him.

Quickly the disciples claimed to have understood everything he was saying (v. 29). Now they felt that he had spoken plainly and not in figures of speech and they had comprehended this meaning. They knew from that explanation that he knew all things. They did not have to question him any further. They had come to the conclusion that he had come from the Father (v. 30). Very blithely they made their confession of faith in him.

Jesus reacted to this easy statement of faith (v. 31). Did they really believe? That belief would be tested; and that testing would not be long in coming. The time would come—in fact, it had already come; his arrest would occur that very night—when they would be scattered. It is not that Jesus questioned the reality of their belief, but he pointed out its limitations. They would scatter and leave him alone. He would face the hour of his greatest trial alone. They could easily and quickly confess their belief in him, but they would have difficulty backing up what they professed by what they practiced. They were not even then totally aware of all that belief in him demanded. But even then, when apparently he would be alone, Jesus would not be all alone. The Father would be with him (v. 32). Throughout his entire life and ministry the Father was with him. And the Father who had been with him throughout the experience of the incarnation would not desert him in his time of deepest need. They would abandon him, but the Father would never abandon him.

He was saying this to them not to scare them but to reassure them (v. 33). They would have the peace that he could give them. There is a contrast in what they have in the world and what they have through him. In the world they have tribulation. In him they have peace. The reason that Jesus can give peace when the world gives tribulation is that he has overcome the world. All that the world can do to a person in rejection and desertion would be done to Jesus. But he would overcome all that. While the cross looked like the defeat of Jesus it was really his victory. The sorrowing heart of the believer in Christ can be cheered, for the one living in Christ lives in his peace.

The High-Priestly Prayer (17:1-26)

Jesus ended the farewell discourse with a prayer. Often called the high-priestly prayer of Jesus, it gets its name from the fact that Jesus assumed the role of the high priest in making intercession for the people and in offering sacrifice for them. The unique element of Jesus offering sacrifice for the people as the high priest is that he was the sacrifice himself (see Heb. 9:11 to 10:14).

Some have thought that this prayer gives the content of Jesus' prayer in the Garden of Gethsemane. By its place in the events of the evening of his arrest and the opening words of chapter 17 it would seem that this is a different prayer from that prayer of submission to God's will Jesus prayed in the Garden of Gethsemane even though John does not record the content of his prayer there.

Likely Jesus voiced this prayer as he and his disciples crossed the Temple area on the way to the Garden of Gethsemane from the upper room. The prayer is divided into three parts. Jesus prayed for himself, his immediate disciples, and his ultimate believers.

A prayer for himself (17:1-5).—When Jesus had finished his statement to the disciples with the assurance that he had overcome the world, he prayed. Apparently, they did not stop as he prayed; the prayer may have been spoken as they continued to walk across the Temple area.

The posture for the prayer was the common gesture of looking toward heaven. The address of the prayer was the familiar term, "Father."

This was the most common form of address of Jesus to God. It also indicated the close personal relationship between Jesus and God. As a child approaches his father who cares for him, comforts him, and counsels him Jesus called upon God, the Father, in prayer (v. 1).

The hour had come. Throughout Jesus' entire ministry he had pointed toward the "hour" when he would be glorified. There was always the consciousness that he operated according to a divine calendar. Even though the cross had not yet occurred, the events that led step-by-step to the cross and his ultimate glorification had already begun. He was in that "hour," and it was as though it had already happened. He had so committed himself to obedient submission to the will of the Father that it could be expressed as though it had already taken place.

In that hour he prayed for mutual glorification. Both the Father and the Son were so closely identified that what would bring glory and praise to one would also bring glory and praise to the other. The world around them would consider the cross an instrument of shame. But for Jesus it would be transformed into a matter of glory. From his death on the cross would come glory: what he was would become evident and God would be praised through it. And as it glorified him it would also glorify the Father (v. 1).

One of the ways in which the Father would be glorified as the Son was glorified was that eternal life could be given to all who believed on Jesus (v. 2). Notice that the power to convey eternal life was given by the Father. And those to whom eternal life was given were given to him by the Father. The work of one was the work of both.

Eternal life is defined (v. 3). To have eternal life is to know by experience the only true God through faith in Jesus Christ. This is a present reality. One cannot know the only true God (a reminder that the Jewish belief in one God was not compromised) without belief on Jesus Christ. And belief in Jesus Christ brought about that experiential knowledge of God. When one knows he believes; when one believes on Jesus Christ he knows God by experience.

Jesus, the Son, had brought glory to God, the Father, while he was on earth by his obedient accomplishment of all that God had given him to do. But then he asked that God would glorify him in his presence with the glory that he had once had (v. 5). The preexistence of Jesus (see 1:1-3) was affirmed. Before his incarnation he had shared the glory of God in heaven. Now as he had completed, or was about to complete, the work God had sent him to the earth to do, he asked once more for the perfect glory that he had known previously. By his incarnation he had voluntarily limited himself as a human being to one time and place. Through his ascension he would be freed from those limitations of person, place, and time and thus could know the unlimited glory he once had.

Jesus consecrated himself to the task before him. He prepared for his death by a complete committal of his life to the Father.

A prayer for his disciples (17:6-19).—As he prayed for his disciples Jesus gave an account of his stewardship with them. He had made the name and character of God known to them (v. 6). These disciples, the followers of Jesus, had been given to him by the Father. As a testimony to them, they had kept the word which Jesus had shared with them. The word referred to all the teaching which Jesus had given them. These were people who had come out of the world surrounding them to accept by faith the witness that Jesus gave of God, the Father. The people knew by experience that what Jesus had revealed to them of God had come from God (v. 7). Jesus was a perfect and adequate witness to God. He and God were identified so closely in his mission that these disciples were convinced that Jesus had come from God, that the teaching of Jesus was the teaching of God, and that by believing on Jesus they were believing on God (vv. 7-8).

In this prayer Jesus did not pray for all the world (v. 9). This did not indicate that he did not love the whole world; it does indicate that in that prayer he was zeroing in on those whom God had given him as believers. These were the people who belonged to God by faith. And they belong mutually to the Father and the Son since they were identified in their purpose (v. 10). Through them Jesus would be glorified. By their continued witness following his death and resurrection people would come to the conclusion that he was indeed the Son of God sent from God. This would glorify Jesus.

But the time was fast approaching when Jesus would no longer be in the world. In fact, this is worded as though it had already happened. Jesus would depart the world in order to be with the Father. But the disciples, his believers, would remain in the world. Since they would be in the world to bear witness to the world, Jesus called on the Father—whom he addressed as Holy Father, that Father which has holiness as his character—to keep them. He could keep them in the power of his own name, which means the power and authority of himself, his person.

As they are preserved in the power of God, Jesus asked for their unity (v. 11). The Father and Son were known separately, but they were identified with one another. They had a unity of purpose. The disciples were separate individuals, but they could have a unity of purpose that centered in Jesus Christ. That Jesus prayed for.

While he had been physically present with them on the earth he could keep them. And he did that. He stood guard over them so that none were lost but Judas whom he identified as "the son of perdition" (v. 12). The son of perdition likely refers to one who was completely given over to evil. The explanation for his loss in the midst of Jesus' claim of protection of his followers is found in Scripture. His defection from the apostolic band was no surprise; it simply bore out the scriptural prediction. Possibly the Scripture references are to Psalm 69:25 or 109:6-8, even though none are cited. As Jesus would leave them to come to the Father he wanted them to know fully his joy. Like his peace, his joy is given as a grace gift of God and supersedes the circumstances of life (v. 13).

Jesus described the position of his disciples in the world. They would know the hatred of the world. The reason was that they were in the world but not of the world. As the world had hated Jesus—even putting him to death—it would follow logically that it would hate his disciples as they followed him. That they had kept the word, the teachings of God given by Jesus, made them different from the world around them (v. 14). But Jesus did not pray that they would be taken out of the world. George W. Truett identified that as the prayer that Jesus refused to pray. He refused to pray that they would be physically removed from the world around them. He did pray that they would be protected from the evil one while in the world (v. 15). The main interest and focus of life of the disciples was not on the world (v. 16). Just as Jesus was different from the world so were they. The world is the place of Christian witness and work. God took the world so seriously that Jesus became a man and came to the world. The most effective Christian witness is not that one is somehow removed from the world. It is, instead, that one, like God, takes the world so seriously that he bears a distinct witness to God while in the world. While living in the world (that is the only place people have to live) the Christian is not totally identified with the goals, attitudes, and life-styles of the world.

Jesus next prayed that his followers would be sanctified in truth. The word *sanctify* means to set apart for God's service. In Jewish thought, persons, places, and things could be sanctified. Here the prayer is that persons who follow Christ in faith should be set apart in truth. Truth is defined as God's word (v. 17). The word about God, the teachings of God, that Jesus had made known were truth. That is what truth is: God's word is the touchstone for truth. It is that truth that cleanses persons (15:3).

These people are being sent into the world as Jesus was sent into the world (v. 18). All Christians live under commission. As Jesus was sent into the world to reveal God and to redeem persons, Christians are sent into the world to make God known and to be redeeming witnesses in the world. Jesus had consecrated himself for that task (v. 19). And he prayed that those who followed him might also be consecrated for the task that God had commissioned them to do. As there is an identification of the Son with the Father in his ministry in the world so is there an identification of the Christians and the Savior in their witnessing and ministering task in the world.

A Prayer for all believers (17:20-26).—Jesus expanded the scope of his prayer from his present disciples to include all believers of all times. This was based on the presumption that his disciples would continue his ministry and witness in the world. Others would believe on him through their word, as they had believed God through his word (v. 20). It is for this expanded circle of Christians that Jesus prayed in the last part of his high-priestly prayer.

The burden of his prayer was for unity (v. 21). He and the Father had a unity even as they had a distinction in person. There would be a lot of new people coming into the new church. They would bring with them differences of temperament, personality, and outlook. But they could have a unity of purpose. This unity of purpose would bring them into identity with the Father and the Son. The purpose of this unity is witness: "so that the world may believe that thou hast sent me" (v. 21). The purpose of the unity was neither organic nor functional but evangelistic. By the observation of the unity of the believers which mirrored the unity of the Father and the Son the world would then believe that the Father had sent the Son. It would be a clear witness to the Christ resulting in belief.

As the identity between the Father and the Son had been shared so would the glory be shared (v. 22). The glory convinces of the presence of God and leads to belief. That, too, would be a result of the unity as well as a mark of the unity. The believers would be marked with the same unity of purpose as seen in Father and Son. In knowing that God loved the believers and sent them, as God loved the Son and sent him, the world would come to a belief in God (v. 23). Notice that the repeated result of both the revelation of God and the resultant unity of believers is belief.

Jesus really would have liked for the disciples to be with him when he came into his glory (v. 24). What they had accepted of him by belief could be proved if they would witness the glory that the Father had given him from the very beginning. Obviously this would not be possible. He had already told them that they could not receive the power of the Holy Spirit without his departure (14:16-17). Also, they would not be able to give witness of their unity with him and with one another if they were not in the world themselves to bear this witness.

In closing the prayer Jesus addressed God as "righteous Father" (v. 25). As he had earlier indicated that God, the Father, had a character of holiness (v. 11), he then indicated that the Father had a nature of righteousness. God was righteous by nature. The world around him had not known the Father. But Jesus knew the Father. His revelation of God was based on his personal knowledge and personal communion with the Father. Those who believed on Jesus knew that he had been sent by the Father.

Jesus had made known the name of the Father, which means that he had made known to them the person, the nature, and the authority of the Father (v. 26). What he had witnessed of the Father would be vindicated, proved true, by his glorification through his death and resurrection. It had been done in love. And the burden of the revelation had been love. Jesus had let them know that God loved them. His fullest desire was that they should know the love of God through him. The same kind of love that God showed to Jesus, Jesus had shown to them. The believers whom Jesus was leaving behind on the earth to continue and to extend his ministry would be included in the circle of love that included both the Father and the Son.

Testimony (18:1-40)

The countdown to the cross continued. As Jesus completed his final instructions to his disciples he went to the Garden of Gethsemane on the Mount of Olives where he was arrested and taken to trial. Truly the hour of his glorification had arrived.

In the next two chapters the account of the last stages of Jesus' life as portrayed by the writer of John's Gospel parallels the Synoptic Gospels' accounts closely. Yet there are some elements found in the Synoptic Gospels—the agony in the garden, the kiss of betrayal, the carrying of his cross, for instance—which are omitted in the Fourth Gospel. At the same time, there are some details—Jesus' voluntary arrest, the discussion with Pilate concerning kingship, and the result of the spear thrust into his side, for instance—that are added by the Fourth Gospel. Throughout this account the impression is definitely given that Jesus was in charge. In the events which showed shame and degradation to the common mind, Jesus acted with regal authority and voluntarily committed himself to the cross in accordance to the Father's will.

Arrest (18:1-11)

When Jesus completed his prayer he went with his disciples across the Kidron Valley to the Mount of Olives (v. 1). From the passage itself it is difficult to determine if Jesus completed the farewell discourse and his high-priestly prayer in the upper room and then departed or if these things were spoken after leaving the upper room en route to the Kidron Valley. The interpretation followed here has been that Jesus spoke these words of the farewell discourse and voiced the high-priestly prayer as he and his group traveled from the upper room to the Kidron Valley. By the time they reached the valley Jesus had completed the sayings recorded and crossing the valley went up the slope of the Mount of Olives to the Garden of Gethsemane.

The Kidron is a winter torrent that runs southward along the east side of the city of Jerusalem. It is dry in the summer but flows during the winter and spring rains.

The writer does not identify the garden to which Jesus and his disciples went. Other Gospel writers identified it as the Garden of Gethsemane. The word *Gethsemane* means "oil press." Likely the garden was an olive grove in which was located an oil press to press the olive oil from the olives produced in the garden. John did not even identify the mountain as the Mount of Olives. This information, too, is supplied by the Synoptics.

Since the garden was familiar to Judas it must have been a place where Jesus and his disciples frequently went. There is the possibility that they camped out there during the time of Passover. Since Jerusalem was crowded at the feast time the area considered the city was expanded to include the environs of the city. Lying on the other side of the Mount of Olives, Bethany, where Jesus often stayed, would not have been considered a part of the city at feast time, while the Garden of Gethsemane would have fallen within that designation. Unable to find or to afford accommodations within the city itself Jesus and his disciples may have spent the evenings camping in the garden. Or it could have simply been a favorite place of Jesus for prayer, meditation, and relaxation.

No matter what reason Jesus went to the garden, Judas knew where to find him (v. 2). Leading a group of Roman soldiers, along with Temple police, Judas led the arresting group directly to Jesus (v. 3). Although there would have been a full moon during the Passover season, they went to the garden equipped with lanterns and torches in case they had to search for Jesus and his followers among the trees in the garden. The number of arresting officers and soldiers led by Judas is not specified. The usual size of a Roman cohort was six hundred men. It would hardly seem that they would need that large a contingent to arrest one unarmed man with eleven followers. They may have feared, however, that he either had a private army secreted away outside the city or that others would quickly spring to his cause. Whatever the actual number of armed people, it was obviously more than really necessary to arrest one man.

And when they came to arrest that man he voluntarily stepped forward, asking whom they sought in the garden. The Synoptic Gospels indicate that Judas betrayed Jesus with a kiss, the common gesture of greeting among friends. The writer of John's Gospel does not include that detail. Instead, carrying out the theme of the voluntariness of Jesus' death he indicated that Jesus stepped forward himself (v. 4).

When they replied that they were seeking Jesus of Nazareth, he responded by identifying himself with the same term, "I am," that he had previously used in his claims (8:24,28,58). At this, the arresting officers fell back in shock. Accustomed to resistance by persons they were arresting, they were possibly shocked by his reaction to them. Also, they may have fallen prostrate at his words because the form of Jesus' identification to them was the language of diety. The arresting officers were literally floored by Jesus' response to them. It was noted that Judas was standing with them. At this point, there was no doubt about which side Judas had chosen (vv. 5-6).

Giving himself up rather than being arrested, Jesus again asked them whom they sought. When they answered once more that they were looking for Jesus of Nazareth, he again identified himself to them. Going further, he even dictated the terms of his surrender to them (vv. 7-8). If he was the one they wanted then they should let the others with him go free. Jesus had already indicated in his prayer that he had not lost any of those the Father had given to him (17:12), and this was being carried out in his request to the arresting soldiers.

One of Jesus' followers, however, was not quite ready to give up so easily. Showing his characteristic of physical courage and moral cowardice, Simon Peter drew a sword and, swinging at the high priest's servant, severed his ear. Unlike the writers of the Synoptic Gospels, the writer of John's Gospel identified both the disciple who took up the sword and the slave who felt the brunt of it. Probably swinging wildly in the dark, Peter was not aiming at the ear but at the head. The slave may even have ducked at the blow and lost his right ear. Luke's Gospel indicates that Jesus healed the servant, replacing the ear (Luke 22:51).

But violence was not Jesus' method. Rebuking Peter, he commanded him to put up the sword. He had to drink the cup the Father had given to him, the cup of suffering and death that would result in the deliverance of all others. His was not an earthly kingdom, and it could not be brought in by violence. Instead, it was a spiritual kingdom that would be realized through obediently following the will of the Father, even if it meant death. Which it did.

Religious Trial (18:12-27)

The trial of Jesus fell into two parts: a religious trial and a civil trial. The religious trial was before the Jewish religious leaders who had already decided that Jesus must die (11:53). That trial, too, was in two parts: one before Annas, a former high priest and the father-in-law of Caiaphas who was the high priest, and another before Caiaphas and the Jewish council. The civil trial was before Pilate, the Roman governor. Only the Romans had the authority to pronounce the death sentence in an occupied territory such as Israel.

The trial before the high priest (18:12-24).—Having arrested Jesus in the Garden of Gethsemane, the arresting officers bound him and carried him to Annas, the former high priest. Jesus had voluntarily given himself up to them, yet they still bound him as though he were a dangerous fugitive (v. 12).

Annas had previously been the high priest but had been deposed by the Romans. A person of considerable authority and power still, however, he had five sons and one son-in-law, Caiaphas, who succeeded him as high priest. So even though Caiaphas actually had the title of high priest at the time of the arrest and trial of Jesus, Annas probably had the power. The writer of John's Gospel identified Annas as Caiaphas' father-in-law. He also made mention of the fact that Caiaphas was the high priest at the time. The reading seems to indicate that the office of high priest changed each year. It did not. Caiaphas served as high priest for eighteen years, one of which was "that year," that fateful year, in which Jesus the Christ was crucified (v. 13).

Caiaphas was also identified by a previous reference (v. 13). It was Caiaphas who in an earlier meeting of the Jewish council to determine the fate of Jesus had observed that it was expedient for one man to die rather than for the whole nation to be destroyed by the Romans (11:49-52). Caiaphas had made that as a political observation. The Gospel writer picked up that political comment and turned it into a spiritual truth. Jesus had indeed died for the nation, and not that nation only but for all persons of all nations (v. 14). What had been a shrewd political observation turned out to be a theological reality. But at that moment Jesus was standing before the Jewish authority as a common criminal. Possibly shackled hand and foot, it looked as though he needed deliverance rather than his being the means of deliverance of all humankind from its bondage.

Jesus had not come to that place alone. Whether the residence or the office of either Annas or Caiaphas is intended as the place where Jesus was taken is not clear. Probably it was the residence of Annas. Caiaphas may have had quarters there also. Or, if it was the high priest's palace, it may have been Caiaphas's residence—and Annas had quarters there where he could exercise his unofficial authority. Peter and an unnamed disciple showed up at the entrance to the court of the high priest's place (v. 15). The unnamed disciple knew the high priest, and apparently was known at his residence, so he easily gained entrance to the courtyard when Jesus was brought there. Identifying this unnamed disciple would only be speculation. Some have guessed John, Lazarus, Nicodemus, or Joseph of Arimathea. Who he actually was is neither known nor necessary to know. He was well enough known in the high priest's house to gain entrance and to arrange for Peter to gain entrance when he was left standing at the doorway (v. 16). Speaking to the slave girl who was the doorkeeper, the unnamed disciple had enough influence for her to give admittance to Peter.

Perhaps as she opened the door or gate for him to enter she asked a question that was actually phrased in such a way that it would have been easy for him to say "no." The question, in fact, was phrased in such a way that "no" was the expected answer. "You are not one of this man's disciples, too, are you?" is the real force of the question. Following the line of least resistance Peter indicated that he was not (v. 17). She obviously had doubts about who she was letting into the courtyard. And Peter answered the simplest way, even though it was the untruthful way, the way of denial.

Since it was cold that night the officers and servants or slaves had made a charcoal fire in the courtyard and were warming themselves around the fire (v. 18). Apparently trying to melt into the crowd, and likely because he was cold too, Peter joined the crowd around the fire, warming himself while Jesus was being subjected to questioning.

In the informal, illegal pretrial hearing before Annas, the former high priest, Jesus was questioned on two issues: his disciples and his teaching (v. 19). Politically sensitive to his position both in leadership of the Jewish people and of leadership allowed by the Romans, Annas was concerned about the movement that Jesus had begun. He was interested in the number of followers that Jesus had. Religiously, it would make a difference in the number of people departing from the orthodox teachings and worship. Politically, it could make a difference if it looked as though either Jewish authorities or Roman rulers would face an uprising.

Annas was also concerned about what Jesus had been teaching. He wanted to know if there had been one teaching for public consumption and another secret teaching that he gave his closest companions. Quite obviously, one of the purposes of the pretrial hearing was to allow the Jewish religious leaders to formulate the charges that they would use against Jesus and to organize their case against him.

Although Annas was not actually the high priest at that time, he was called by the title in verse 19. This was probably used in the same manner that a former president or governor is always addressed as president or governor. That Annas conducted this hearing seems evident from his action in sending Jesus bound to Caiaphas after the hearing (v. 24).

The reply of Jesus was that Annas did not have to ask him that question. He had taught openly in the Temple and in the synagogues. What they heard was what he had taught. He did not have one set of teachings that he used in public and another in private. He had said nothing privately; it had all been open to all the world to hear (v. 20).

Then Jesus corrected the legal authorities on their legal procedure. A person was not required in Jewish law to incriminate himself. The case was to be established by witnesses. But he was asking Jesus to witness against himself. If Annas were really interested in knowing what Jesus taught he could ask witnesses. They had heard him express his teachings publicly and openly. And they could witness as to what he had taught. The case was evidently prejudiced from the start.

This reply struck one of the officers as arrogant and impudent. Striking Jesus across the face, he showed by the question that he asked that this was not the way he felt one should address the high priest (v. 22).

Still in control of himself and the situation, Jesus asked the officer why he had hit him (v. 23). If Jesus had spoken wrongfully they should have produced the witnesses to disprove what he had said. But if his reply had been truthful, which it was, there was no reason to hit him. Violent force would neither serve to change his answer nor to disprove his position.

But neither Annas nor the officer were interested in justice. They had already decided the verdict. All they needed to decide was what argument they would use and how it would be presented. Completing his inquiry, Annas turned Jesus over to the high priest who would conduct the next phase of the trial. Where Jesus would have to go to appear before Caiaphas was not spelled out. Possibly it was in the same building; certainly it was close by. Neither does John's Gospel detail the events in the trial before Caiaphas. The Synoptic Gospels have to be consulted for what happened there.

Peter's denial (18:25-27).—The stage had already been set for Peter's denial of Jesus (vv. 15-18). Jesus had predicted earlier that before daybreak Peter would deny him three times (13:38) even though Peter had boasted that he would even be willing to follow him to the death (13:37).

While still warming himself around the charcoal fire in the courtyard Peter was further questioned about his relationship to Jesus. The other servants there seem to have taken up the question asked by the slave girl who served as the gatekeeper. They, too, phrased the question in such a way that a negative answer was anticipated when they asked Peter if he were a disciple of Jesus. Again, he answered negatively (v. 25).

But once this subject was pursued one person, at least, was not willing to give it up. This slave of the high priest was also a relative of Malchus, the high priest's slave whose ear Peter had cut off in the garden. The light was probably uncertain in the garden and was not too bright around a charcoal fire, but he still thought he recognized Peter as the man who had wielded the sword. He asked Peter directly if he had not seen him in the garden with Jesus. This time the question was phrased in such a way that an affirmative answer was expected (v. 26). But Peter's answer was again negative. He denied that he had been in the garden with Jesus (v. 27).

And with this denial the cock crowed. Jesus had told Peter earlier that evening that before the night was over he would deny him three times. And he had. Showing physical courage in the garden when he tried to protect Jesus by hacking away at Malchus, Peter had shown moral cowardice in the courtyard when he tried to protect himself from the questions of a little slave girl. What a contrast Peter's lack of courage was to the demonstration of courage shown by Jesus before the high priest. There is also a contrast in the reaction of Peter and Judas to their actions. After his betrayal of Jesus, Judas fell into despair and took his own life (Acts 1:18). After his denial of Jesus, Peter was moved to repentance and returned to Jesus. If the place where Jesus was questioned was indeed the residence of both Annas and Caiaphas it could have been while Jesus was being taken from Annas to Caiaphas in separate quarters that he passed through the courtyard and looked at Peter following the third denial (Luke 22:61).

Civil Trial (18:28-40)

Accusation to Pilate (18:28-32).—The details of the trial before Caiaphas are not given. Jesus was then brought from the house of the high priest to the residence of the Roman governor, the praetorium (v. 28). The praetorium refers to the entire complex of the governor's residence, the military barracks, and the judgment hall. It may have been connected with the Tower of Antonio just beyond the Temple area or connected with Herod's palace. There is some thought that Pilate, the governor, may have actually stayed at Herod's palace during the feast time in Jerusalem. The Roman governor actually lived at the praetorium in Caesarea.

This transfer occurred early in the morning. Since they were still at the high priest's house at cockcrow and they had followed that with the trial before Caiaphas, the events must have progressed rather rapidly one after another.

Interestingly enough, the Jewish authorities who had shattered their own legal procedures in the arrest and trial of Jesus were so fastidious religiously that they would not enter the praetorium. That very evening they expected to eat the Passover meal. They would not risk religious contamination by entering a Gentile building. They thought nothing of demanding the death of an innocent man.

Willing to accommodate the Jewish rulers, Pilate went out to meet them since they would not come in the building before him (v. 29). Pilate is introduced rather abruptly into the story without any identification of his position or any background about his character. Apparently the Gospel writer assumed that all would know that Pilate was the Roman governor at the time.

Pilate had one question for them: what was the accusation against Jesus? The Jewish authorities were not willing to answer that question directly. Instead, they evaded answering the question by asking Pilate a question: if he were not an evildoer would they even have brought him before Pilate? Since Pilate had cooperated in Jesus' arrest by the use of his soldiers they must have assumed that Pilate would also cooperate in his sentencing. Blasphemy had been their charge against Jesus religiously. But that would not hold up in a Roman court. It would have to be a charge with political overtones. Ultimately, they settled on treason as the charge.

Thinking that it was some religious dispute or some Jewish matter that they had in mind, Pilate told them to judge him according to their own law. The Romans allowed a great deal of latitude among the people they ruled in deciding their own religious matters.

But the Jewish leaders were not satisfied with that answer. They reminded Pilate that they could not pronounce the death sentence (v. 31). They wanted Jesus executed. None of the things that they could decide would allow them to execute him in the way they had in mind. The Jews generally put people to death by stoning. The Roman method of execution was by crucifixion. A death by crucifixion would completely discredit Jesus, and their rejection of him would be justified.

In an interpretive statement, the writer of the Fourth Gospel indicated that this fulfilled the prediction that Jesus himself had made about the way he would die (v. 32). Jesus had earlier said that he would be "lifted up" (12:32), which was taken as an indication that he would die by crucifixion. Since the Jews executed by stoning, his death would have to be at Roman hands if by crucifixion. The Jewish

Law in Deuteronomy had stated that one hanged on a tree was cursed (Deut. 21:23). Caiaphas would see death by crucifixion as the way that Jesus would be thoroughly discredited; John saw it as the way that Jesus took away the sin of the world.

Questioning by Pilate (18:33-38a).—Going back into the praetorium, Pilate called Jesus to come to him. The religious leaders would not enter the praetorium. Jesus had neither scruples against it nor choice in the matter.

There Pilate asked him a question: was he the king of the Jews (v. 33)? Evidence has not yet been introduced into John's Gospel of the charge that the religious leaders would lodge against Jesus. They were convinced of his blasphemy. But that would be quickly dismissed by Pilate, as he had already tried to do (v. 31). From this question and the response of the crowd in 19:12 it becomes apparent that the Jews had used the charge of treason against Jesus. They had accused him of being a revolutionary who would try to set up a kingship to rival that of Caesar's. While the Roman authorities could give some latitude in the conduct of its own affairs to a subject nation, they would not countenance rivals to Caesar's throne. The prisoner before him did not look like a king to Pilate.

Jesus immediately turned the tables on Pilate. In Jesus' question to Pilate as a response to Pilate's question to him, there is an evident shift of power (v. 34). The questioned becomes the questioner. The initiative is taken out of the hands of Pilate and is assumed by Jesus, who was supposed to have been on trial before Pilate. Jesus wanted to know where Pilate had come up with that question. Was it a conclusion at which he had arrived by weighing the evidence? Or was it a trumped-up charge that had been suggested to him by the religious leaders who were trying to do him in?

Contemptuously, Pilate asked if he were a Jew who would have to answer questions from this king of the Jews (v. 35). The question that was Pilate's retort could also mean that since he was not a Jew he could not answer questions concerning Jewish kingship. But then he went on to add that the chief priests had handed Jesus over to him. What had he done that would cause them to do this?

Jesus did not answer that question directly but instead dealt with the matter of kingship. He replied that his kingship was not of the world (v. 36). If his kingship were of the world he would have an army as the world's kings that would fight against his being delivered to Pilate by the chief priests. But his kingship was not from the world. It was an entirely different kind of kingship from that which comes from the world or is known by the world.

Seizing on that, Pilate replied, "So you are a king?" (v. 37). Pilate may have seen what looked to him like an opening. Maybe there was something to their charge after all.

But Jesus' answer again turned the decision to Pilate. It was Pilate that had pronounced him king. And as further explanation of the nature of his kingship Jesus said that the reason that he was born into the world, the reason that he came into the world, was to bear witness to the truth. Pilate would not have caught the reference to his coming into the world. But the very purpose of Jesus' coming into the world was to bear witness of the truth. Those who are of truth are the ones that hear his voice and respond to him. His kingdom is a kingdom of truth.

Perhaps wistfully, possibly jestingly, maybe with a shrug, Pilate asked, "What is truth?" (v. 38) and ended the interview. Pilate did not wait to get the answer to his question. He probably did not think he could get the answer from the prisoner before him. While Pilate did not wait for the answer to his question, and Jesus did not put an answer in words, it does not mean that there is no answer to it. The events of the death and resurrection of Jesus give the answer to that question. On the cross and at the empty tomb God's truth is seen. But Pilate did not really want to know the answer. It was his way of dismissing the subject and ending the interview.

Offer of release: Jesus or Barabbas (18:38b-40).—Finding out what he wanted to know—that Jesus was no revolutionary and claimant to the Roman throne—Pilate went out of the praetorium again (v. 38). Apparently by this time a crowd had gathered. The crowd, in fact, may have been gathered up by the Jewish leaders. Addressing the crowd, and not the Jewish leaders who had brought Jesus to him, Pilate announced that he could find Jesus guilty of no crime.

But in an effort to get himself off the hook, Pilate brought up a custom that is not mentioned anywhere except in the Gospels, the custom of releasing a criminal at the feast time. Likely he thought that he would placate the rulers by calling Jesus a criminal. And if the people chose to release Jesus it would not be he but their own people who had given him freedom. But if they chose another to release, which apparently Pilate did not anticipate, he would not have personally pronounced the sentence on a man that he considered innocent.

Likely with sarcasm or scorn in his voice Pilate asked the people if they would like for him to release for them the king of the Jews (v. 39). He probably thought that the sentiment of the crowd would be for Jesus and against the priests and that they would accept his offer of the release of Jesus.

Instead they cried out for the release of Barabbas (v. 40). In the first reference to any response or cry of the crowd they called for the release of Barabbas rather than the release of Jesus.

In an explanatory reference it is noted that Barabbas was a robber. The word used indicates that Barabbas was an insurrectionist, a rebel, an outlaw more than a petty thief. If this was true, he may have been a local hero for leading resistance against the Romans and was being held for execution. From the account of John's Gospel it seems that the crowd themselves, perhaps at someone's instigation, suggested Barabbas as the one who should be released. In an ironic twist to Pilate's offer, a real revolutionary was being released rather than one against whom that charge was falsely lodged.

Another irony is seen in his name. The name Barabbas means "son of the father." One who was simply called son of the father was being released while that one who was the true Son of the Father would go to his death.

If Pilate wanted a criminal to release at the feast he got a real criminal while the innocent one was sent to the cross. Truly this was a king that Pilate could not understand.

Termination (19:1-42)

The termination of Jesus' earthly life was at hand. Brought before the Roman governor, Pilate, Jesus had been peremptorily tried and found guilty by the Jews, but Pilate had difficulty in seeing his guilt. Making attempts to satisfy them without executing Jesus, Pilate failed each time. Reacting to their accusation that Jesus claimed to be a king and their threat to report Pilate to Rome for failing to deal with a revolutionary who claimed the throne, Pilate allowed Jesus to be crucified.

Condemnation (19:1-16)

Failing in his attempt to have Jesus released by the demand of the crowd for the release of Barabbas, Pilate had Jesus scourged (v. 1). Possibly he thought that the sight of the blood and the viciousness of the punishment would satisfy their thirst for blood. With that punishment, Pilate probably reasoned, they would be satisfied and Jesus could be released. But that tactic did not work either.

The scourging was traditionally done just prior to crucifixion. The scourge was a whip of several thongs with bits of metal or bone at the ends of each lash. Rendered with the strong arm of a Roman soldier, the scourging itself would lay bare the back of the victim. Often the scourging brought on death before the crucifixion could be carried out.

Whether Pilate had Jesus rigged up with the mock crown and purple robe to ridicule the idea of his kingship or this was spontaneous horseplay by the soldiers is not clear. Pilate did take advantage of it to ridicule Jesus before the crowd. From some sort of thorny branches the soldiers plaited a crown which they pressed on Jesus' head, with the thorns cutting into his head. A crown of honor was sometimes fashioned in which spikes radiated upward from the crown. The spikes in Jesus' crown radiated downward and dug into his head. The robe was likely a purple robe worn by a Roman officer. Purple was the color of royalty.

Wearing a crown and a purple robe Jesus was further ridiculed and mocked by the soldiers as they came before him with a royal salute and salutation, "Hail, King of the Jews!" (v. 3). They also hit him with their fists and struck him with open hands, perhaps even backhanding him.

While the flogging may have been public, the horseplay was apparently out of view of the crowd. Pilate then went out before the people, again bringing Jesus with him (v. 4). He announced to them that he was bringing Jesus out to them because he had not found him guilty of any crime. As Jesus came before them wearing the crown of thorns and the cast-off purple robe, with sarcasm Pilate said, "Behold the man!" (v. 5).

Pilate said more than he realized in that statement. Probably meaning it sarcastically, he presented them with the man they had charged with claiming to be king. Beaten, bloody, ridiculed, dressed in a ridiculous parody of kingship, he did not much look like a king then. But Pilate was also presenting to them *the* Man; the man whose favorite title for himself was Son of man; the man who came from God and was sent from God into the world; the man who made God known to the people of the world; the man whose death would bring deliverance and forgiveness of sin to all persons of the world. Indeed, here is the man!

But the Jewish leaders were not impressed with either the man or Pilate's presentation of him. Immediately the chief priests and the religious authorities cried out to crucify him. Literally it is one word: "Crucify! Crucify!" And the chant may have been taken up by the crowd. Notice, however, that it was begun by the religious authorities (v. 6).

Seeing that his second attempt to satisfy the people and to free Jesus had failed, Pilate said sarcastically to them that if they wanted him to be crucified they would have to crucify him themselves (v. 6). Pilate did not find him guilty of any crime that would deserve crucifixion. In fact, he did not find him guilty of any crime at all. Three times he had told them that he found Jesus innocent (18:36; 19:4,6).

The Jewish leaders gave a serious answer to Pilate's sarcastic rejoinder. It was not that they did not want to crucify him, but they could not crucify him. The Romans would not let them. And their method of execution was stoning, not crucifixion. They appealed to their own Jewish law in which it was stated that anyone claiming to be God, or trying to make himself equal to God, should be executed (v. 7). They were resorting to the law against blasphemy as stated in Leviticus 24:16. And at that point they showed their hand. The business about claiming to be king was all a smoke screen to bring the Roman authority into the execution. Their real concern was a religious concern. It was his religious claims that had antagonized and angered them. If Pilate could not find him guilty on his terms, let him look at him from their standpoint. Again, unwittingly, they had identified Jesus as exactly what he in fact was: the Son of God. This was not the first time they had accused him of this (5:18; 8:53; 10:33). And he had been confessed as the Son of God previously (11:27).

Pilate was a bit shaken by this. The Romans were full of stories of gods who had consorted with humans and whose offspring performed wondrous deeds. Though he may have been more superstitious than believing, Pilate did not want to take any chances of offending a son of a god. Besides, he possibly had his wife's dream fresh on his mind (Matt. 27:19). Taking Jesus back into the praetorium, Pilate again questioned Jesus (vv. 8-9). This time he had one direct question: where did Jesus come from?

But Jesus refused to answer Pilate's question. In regal dignity and silence he stood before the somewhat frightened Roman governor. This infuriated Pilate. He then asked Jesus if he did not realize that he had the power of life and death. It was within Pilate's power to either crucify Jesus or to release him (v. 10).

Jesus did have a reply to that. Jesus told him that he did not have any power over Jesus that had not been granted from above, that is, from God. The power above him to which Jesus referred was not the power of the Roman emperor or senate but of God. The whole affair was in the hands of God. And because of that, the greater guilt for his death would be upon the Jewish authorities who delivered Jesus to Pilate rather than upon Pilate himself (v. 11). Once again, Jesus showed that he was in control of the situation in which Pilate had thought him only the victim.

Satisfied with Jesus' penetrating analysis of the situation, Pilate sought once more to release Jesus (v. 12). Repeatedly, he had tried to let this innocent man go free. But again he was shouted down by the demand to crucify Jesus.

This time the Jewish leaders gave a veiled threat that Pilate felt he could not ignore. They said that if Jesus were set free Pilate would not be Caesar's friend, for any person who set himself up as a king would oppose Caesar, the Roman emperor (v. 12). Caesar's friend may have been a technical term which applied to those persons who were the close and chosen friends of the emperor. This may have been a position that Pilate desired but had not attained. Or the term could have simply referred to the matter of Pilate's loyalty to Caesar and to the government which employed him. With high treason as the charge against Jesus, Pilate could hardly afford to ignore it. Pilate got the message.

Bringing Jesus out before them again, Pilate sat down, which was the normal position for pronouncing a sentence (v. 13). The place where he sat was called "The Pavement"; it could have been where judgment was usually pronounced at the praetorium. The Hebrew word for it was *Gabbatha,* which means "the ridge." It was possibly some sort of high place. The politician had overtaken the person. Even though he personally had considered Jesus innocent, as a politician he could not ignore the threats of the Jewish leaders.

John noted the day and date carefully (v. 14). It was the day prior to the Passover, which would begin at sundown that day. It was at about noon by the Roman method of reckoning time. The ordeal had started very early in the morning, somewhere near daybreak. According to John's Gospel Jesus' sentence would be pronounced at about the same time Jewish families would be preparing the lamb they would slaughter for the Passover meal. His death would occur at about the time the lamb would actually be slain.

Once more Pilate presented Jesus in a satirical manner when he presented the beat up and bloody man to them as their king (v. 14). And once more Pilate had said more than he was aware. Jesus was indeed the King, in fact, the King of kings, even though he would not appear so to a cynical Roman politician whose best impulses had been debased that day. But this king had acted in regal fashion all of that bleak day.

And also once more the Jewish people shouted Pilate down. They wanted Jesus crucified, and that was what they shouted. They wanted no part of him as a king. Their desire was for him to be taken away and crucified.

Mockingly Pilate asked if he should crucify their king. Defiantly they answered back that they had no king but Caesar (v. 15). Normally that would have been the last thing they would have said. Fiercely independent, claiming to exist under God's rule alone, they would not normally pledge that kind of allegiance to Rome. But this day they needed Rome. This day they wanted Rome to do their bloody work. And in a cynical reply, which the cynical Pilate recognized for what it was, they claimed allegiance to Caesar alone.

Then Pilate handed Jesus over to them to be crucified (v. 16). To whom did he hand Jesus for crucifixion? He handed him to the Jews in the sense that they had prevailed that day. Against Pilate's better judgment and his sense of Roman justice they had prevailed. They won. Pilate was sure of Jesus' innocence and persisted in his attempts to free him, but the Jewish authorities found the key to unlock his will. In the end, they won over Pilate, and he handed Jesus over to them for crucifixion. What they had resolved to do much earlier would actually be accomplished.

But it was literally to the Roman soldiers that Pilate handed Jesus for crucifixion. Theirs would be the responsibility for carrying out that which the Jews had arranged and to which Pilate acceded.

The account in John's Gospel does not show Pilate actually pronouncing a sentence of judgment against Jesus. Worn down and defeated, he may have just assented to the uproarious demands of the people and turned Jesus over to the soldiers for execution.

Crucifixion (19:17-37)

The execution detail of the Roman soldiers took Jesus to the place of execution. Normally an execution detail consisted of four legionnaires and a centurion. Considering the number of parts into which Jesus' garments were divided, apparently this was the number of soldiers directly involved in his death.

As was customary with those convicted, Jesus carried the crossbar of his cross himself. John's account does not mention Simon of Cyrene carrying the cross for him part of the way. The writer of John's Gospel emphasized throughout that Jesus' death was voluntary and that he acted by himself.

Jesus was crucified at a place called Golgotha in the Hebrew. The word means "skull," but why it was called that is not really known. It could have been because it was a skull-shaped hill. Even though *Calvary* (the Latin word for it) has popularly been thought of as a hill, there is nothing in the account to indicate that it was. It could have been because of the skulls of previously crucified persons lying around. Due to the Jewish aversion to unburied bodies, however, that is unlikely. So actually as the exact location for Calvary is unknown so is the exact reason for its name.

John's Gospel shows restraint in describing the crucifixion. It simply states that Jesus was crucified (v. 18). Crucifixion was a terrible, torturing kind of death. Roman citizens were not crucified. It was practiced only on slaves and foreigners. Death often took up to thirty-six hours or more, since no vital organs were affected by the placing of a person on a cross and securing him there by driving nails through the hands or wrists and feet. Completely stripped, the body hung at torturous positions, and breathing and heart action became increasingly difficult. In addition, the victim was exposed to the weather. A more lingering, painful, humiliating, kind of death could hardly be imagined.

Two criminals were executed with Jesus. Jesus was placed in the middle position (v. 18). The author of John made no further mention of the criminals or of the reason for their execution.

Commonly a sign was erected to show why the individual had been executed. Pilate had a sign written in three languages—Hebrew (actually Aramaic), the language of the people, Latin, the official language of the empire, and Greek, the language of commerce and communication—explaining the death of Jesus (vv. 19-20). The sign proclaimed: "Jesus of Nazareth, the King of the Jews." The Jewish authorities protested at this, saying that it ought to read that he had claimed to be king of the Jews. Adamantly refusing to change it, Pilate said that what he had written would remain (v. 22). Why should they protest? They had charged Jesus with that claim. When it worked to their advantage to make Pilate think that Jesus had claimed to be king they would go along with it. But Pilate had the last word of ridicule. What a ridiculous sight that was: the king of the Jews crucified with common criminals.

Once more Pilate had proclaimed more than he realized. Jesus was not only king of the Jews but of all people. And that fact was proclaimed in a multilingual sign which showed the universality of his kingship.

Usually the soldiers who performed an execution divided the belongings of the executied person among them. In this case there were five items: probably a headdress, a girdle or sash, an outer cloak, sandals, and a tunic worn as an undergarment which was woven of one piece rather than being made of several pieces of cloth sewed together. Obviously, there were four soldiers involved, as they divided the items among themselves. But rather than tearing the tunic into pieces they gambled to see who got it. This was taken as a fulfillment of Psalm 22:18 which was early used by Christians as a prophecy of the crucifixion (vv. 23-24).

Jesus was not totally alone during his crucifixion. In addition to the four unbelieving soldiers, there were four believing women. They were: his mother Mary; his mother's sister, usually assumed to be Salome the wife of Zebedee and the mother of James and John (see Matt. 27:56; Mark 15:40); Mary, Clopas's wife, often thought to be the mother of James the Younger and Joses; and Mary Magdalene, who is sometimes presented as a loose woman helped by Jesus, though there is no New Testament evidence for that assessment of her character (v. 25).

Even in his suffering and humiliation Jesus had compassion and concern for others. Seeing his mother in the anguished group he commended her to that follower designated only as "the disciple whom he loved" for protection and provision. To that disciple he gave the responsibility for her care. Obedient to the Savior, from that time the disciple took Jesus' mother in his care. Perhaps he even took her from the scene of death at that time (vv. 25-27). The author noted that his care for her began immediately.

One of the excruciating elements in death by crucifixion was thirst. Jesus did not forego the pain normally experienced in this kind of death. He, too, thirsted, and he said so. The soldiers soaked a sponge in a bowl of vinegar, actually a cheap vinegary wine, and lifted it to his parched lips (v. 29). He had refused the drugged wine (Mark 15:23; Matt. 27:34) that he might be clearheaded and in control, but this was a different variety. Whether the soldiers gave him the sponge on a javelin or a branch of hyssop, a small bushy plant that was connected to the Passover, is not clear. If it was hyssop, which is what the text indicates even though the word for javelin is very similar, it would further carry out the relationship between Jesus and the death of the lamb at Passover. His thirst was connected with the statement of Psalm 69:21.

With this he uttered one word—"Finished!"—bowed his head and yielded to death (v. 30). The one word, translated "It is finished," indicated that his life was finished; but, more than that, his *work* was completed. What God had sent him into the world to do he had finished by his death on the cross. By John's account, Jesus died on the day the lamb would have been slain for use in the Passover meal. And he died of his own will.

Those who had been so concerned with religious scruples that they would not enter the praetorium (18:28) were also concerned about the defilement of leaving a dead body on a cross overnight (Deut. 21:22-23). The sabbath would begin at sundown, and this would also be the Passover. So they asked Pilate to hasten the deaths by breaking the legs of those crucified (v. 31). The trauma of the blow to the legs as well as the inability to hold any of the weight by the legs would make death come quicker. They had no scruples against defiling persons.

The soldiers did break the legs of the criminals crucified with Jesus (vv. 32-33). But when they came to Jesus they saw that he was already dead and did not break his legs. One of the soldiers, however, either to prove Jesus' death or as a last act of brutality, thrust his spear in Jesus' side. From the wound came both blood and water (v. 34). This shows that an actual human being had suffered an actual death. This was no charade; it was for real. Some significance is often seen also in the fact that both blood and water came from the wound. Earlier in the Gospel both blood and water had been used as terms to express the giving and sustaining of eternal life (see 2:7-9; 3:5; 4:14; 6:53-56; 7:38-39; 13:5-10). Real blood and water came from the wound of the crucified Christ, but this also shows that he is the source of that which nourishes and sustains those who believe on him.

The spear thrust was verified by an eyewitness who was not identified (v. 35). That this happened was true. But it was also taken as scriptural fulfillment of Exodus 12:46; Numbers 9:12; Psalm 34:20, and Zechariah 12:10 (vv. 36-37).

Completion (19:38-42)

With his death, the burial of Jesus would be necessary. Without the intervention of Joseph and Nicodemus, Jesus' body likely would have been tossed into a common pit with the bodies of the other two victims. But two men who had been unwilling to publicly declare for Jesus in his life claimed his body at his death.

Nothing else in John's Gospel is said about Joseph of Arimathea other than that he was a secret disciple of Jesus. From other accounts it is learned that he was rich (Matt. 27:57), that he was a member of the council, the Sanhedrin, who yearned for the kingdom of God (Mark 15:42-46), and that he had not concurred in the vote of the council to condemn Jesus (Luke 23:50-56). Obviously he had ready access to Pilate, from whom he requested Jesus' body (v. 38). Pilate granted that request.

Joseph was assisted by Nicodemus, who had earlier met Jesus at night (3:1-15) and who had defended him before the council (7:45-52). It is interesting that the disciples who had followed Jesus openly during his life fled at his death, and those who had followed him secretly during his life declared themselves at his death.

Joseph and Nicodemus took a hundred pounds of a mixture of the spices myrrh and aloes and put it on his body, wrapping the body in strips of linen cloths (vv. 39-40). This protection of the body from the odors of death was a burial custom of the Jews. This contrasted with the Egyptian custom of embalming and the Roman practice of cremation. The amount of spices used was appropriate for a royal burial.

Close to the place of execution there was a garden. In this garden was a tomb hewn out of solid rock belonging to Joseph of Arimathea (Matt. 27:60). It had never been used. Since it was near sundown by then they quickly buried Jesus in that borrowed tomb (vv. 41-42).

Triumph (20:1-31)

Jesus was crucified on a Friday. Counting as the Jews reckoned time by counting any portion of a day as a day, the resurrection occurred on Sunday, the third day. The earthly life of Jesus was terminated on Friday by his death by crucifixion. But on Sunday, the third day, the first Easter, Jesus triumphed over death, evil, and the apparent power of Roman and Jewish rulers by his resurrection from the dead. He had acted with regal authority throughout his arrest and trial. Through his resurrection he confirmed his triumph over all the adverse powers and authorities that could be arrayed against him. Human tragedy was turned into divine triumph.

Resurrection (20:1-18)

The accounts of the resurrection in the Synoptic Gospels and the Gospel of John differ in the events recounted. No attempt is made here to reconcile the accounts into a continuous narrative. Rather, the witness of the writer of John's Gospel to the resurrection will be examined. Taken together, the varying accounts by the four Gospel writers show the spontaneous nature of the resurrection accounts. There was no attempt on their part to put together an official resurrection account.

An empty tomb (20:1-10).—The Jewish week ended with the sabbath, Saturday. So the first day of the week would be Sunday. On the first day of the week following the death of Jesus on Friday and the Passover observance on Saturday, the sabbath, the followers of Jesus came to his tomb to complete the proper procedures for the burial of his body. The Synoptic accounts mention other women. John's Gospel mentions only Mary Magdalene, which does not necessarily indicate that others were not present with her.

Nicodemus and Joseph of Arimathea had prepared Jesus' body for burial. Mary Magdalene may not have been aware of that preparation. Or there may have been some other common procedures for the proper burial of a body that were not carried out since his body was buried hastily on Friday afternoon before the onset of the sabbath at sundown.

Before daybreak Mary Magdalene went to the borrowed tomb in which Jesus' body had been placed (v. 1). The opening of the tomb, which had probably been hewn from solid rock in a hillside, was covered with a large wheel-shaped stone which ran in a groove. When Mary arrived at the tomb she discovered that the stone had been rolled aside. The door to the tomb stood open.

The Passover sabbath had obviously not been a joyful observance for the disciples of Jesus. Filled with grief and despair, they may have spent it together. Mary Magdalene seemed to know where they were. And she seemed to assume that Simon Peter was the leader of the group. The unnamed beloved disciple heard the report also.

Running from the tomb (could the other women have stayed at the tomb?), Mary gave a breathless and breathtaking report: "they have taken the Lord out of the tomb, and we do not know where they have laid him" (v. 2).

Obviously Mary had not expected a resurrection from the dead. And apparently at the time she gave her first report she did not suspect a resurrection. All she knew was that the body of Jesus was not in the tomb. She felt that someone must have removed the body from the tomb. Who could it have been? It could have been grave robbers. That was a common practice. Or it could have been the Jewish leaders who definitely did not want a shrine where his followers could gather.

Notice, too, that Mary said "we" did not know where they had put the body. Evidently, she expected that the body had been put somewhere. The "we" could have been an editorial we, of course. But probably it referred to the other women not named by the writer of John's Gospel who were with her at the tomb at daybreak, the earliest time they could have started their task.

Peter and the unnamed beloved disciple started toward the tomb (v. 3). They may have started walking and then have broken into a run. Or they could have begun their trip by running since Mary Magdalene had come running to them (v. 4). The other disciple beat Peter to the tomb but only looked into the tomb and did not enter it. What he saw when he looked in the tomb were the undisturbed graveclothes, the cloths which had been used to wrap Jesus' body for burial (v. 5).

Not hesitating at the entrance to the tomb, as had the beloved disciple, Peter burst into the grave. He, too, saw that the grave-clothes were undisturbed. The linen cloths that had been wrapped around Jesus were still lying there in the same configuration, as though the body had simply passed through them. Even the napkin that had been wrapped turban-like around the head was in a separate place as though the head had been elevated on a ledge or a rock used as a pillow (vv. 6-7). Then the other disciple followed Peter into the tomb and saw the same things Peter had observed.

For the beloved disciple this was enough for faith. He believed that Jesus had been raised from the dead. What he saw confirmed a belief in the resurrection for him (v. 8). Later, the early Christians would find in the Old Testament Scriptures passages that they interpreted as teaching the resurrection of the Christ. The resurrection would be proved to them scripturally in this way. But before this search of the Scripture had been made, before this scriptural confirmation of the resurrection had been devised, the beloved disciple believed in the risen Lord (v. 9). What he had seen was enough to convince him: Christ the Lord had risen!

The disciples then returned to their home (v. 10). The first witness to the resurrection was startling indeed. Mary Magdalene was a woman. A woman's testimony was considered inferior to a man's testimony, and, besides, two witnesses were usually needed to verify a report. Mary had been cured by Jesus of a severe malady (Luke 8:2), the possession of demons, which would itself have made her suspect as a witness. And she was from Magdala, a Galilean town known for its immorality. Although she has been described as an immoral woman, there is no biblical evidence for that charge. She was, however, a single individual into whose life Jesus had come, who bore witness to a stupendous event: Jesus had risen! Forgiven sinners, reclaimed persons make good witnesses to the Christ.

***A risen Lord** (20:11-18).*—The two disciples returned to their homes. Mary, apparently arriving later than they did, stayed weeping at the tomb (v. 11). Apparently she had not actually entered the tomb earlier. This time she went into the tomb itself and saw two angels sitting on the shelf where the body of Jesus had been laid (v. 12). There is no indication of how, or whether, she knew they were angels. They questioned why she was crying. She answered that her Lord had been taken away and she did not know where his body had been put (v. 13).

Then, for some reason, she turned around and saw Jesus standing there. Not recognizing him, possibly because of poor light, because her eyes were clouded by tears, or due to her lack of concentration, she thought that he was the gardener. He, too, asked her why she was crying and whom she sought. Possibly thinking that the gardener had removed the body because he did not want an executed criminal buried in his garden, she asked where he had carried Jesus' body. Without any suggestion as to how she would do it, she said that she would take the body away herself (vv. 14-16).

Jesus then spoke her name, "Mary." At the sound of his voice and the mention of her name she recognized him. She called him "Rabboni," which was really more than teacher; it was a word that meant "my dear lord" and was often used in prayer. She apparently hugged him or fell at his feet to wrap her arms around his legs (v. 16). But Jesus told her to quit holding him, or perhaps to stop clinging to him. Then he told her why she should stop clinging to him. He had not yet ascended to the Father. He gave her a message to take to the disciples, called here his "brethren." That message was that Jesus would ascend to the Father, to God (v. 17).

In clinging to Jesus Mary had sought to hold Jesus in the old relationship. But that relationship would be changed. She could not hold him to the earth and confine him to the previous relationship alone. He would ascend to the Father and thus would have a relationship of Savior and Lord to all the world. She had to release him for that, but John does not record it.

But the new relationship was expressed also in the message Jesus gave her to carry to the disciples. He would ascend; they needed to know that, too. But notice that in his ascension he would ascend to "*my* father and *your* father, to *my* God and *your* God" (author's italics). Through their resurrected Savior, Jesus, the disciples and all believing people have a relationship to God as Father and God. The relationship of Jesus to God as Father was unique because he was the only-one-of-his kind Son of God (3:16). But by faith all believing people become a part of God's family as children of God (1:12). Notice, too, that Jesus called them neither servants (13:16) nor friends (15:15) but brothers.

This time as Mary returned to the disciples her witness had more content. She knew the Lord had risen rather than thinking his body had been removed. She had both seen him and talked with him. And she told them what he had said to her (v. 18).

Reassurance (20:19-29)

In other appearances to the believing group the risen Lord gave further reassurance to his disciples. In these appearances he began to fulfill what he had promised them in the farewell discourses (ch. 13—17). These reassuring appearances proved the continuity and identity of the earthly Jesus with the risen Lord.

To the group of followers (20:19-23).—With a characteristic reference to the time, the writer of John's Gospel indicated that on the evening of the resurrection day the followers of Jesus were gathered behind closed doors. The implication is that the group of believers was larger than the eleven apostles. They were frightened of the Jewish leaders, now that it was known that the body of Jesus was not in the tomb. They knew that he had been resurrected. But would the Jewish authorities believe that?

Suddenly Jesus was right there with them (v. 19). The nature of the resurrection body apparently was such that the closed doors presented no obstacle to him. His word was the characteristic Hebrew greeting, "Peace," but it must have carried more content with it that evening. Having greeted them, he showed them his hands and his side to prove to them that they were seeing the same Jesus they had seen on the cross. They were very glad to see him (v. 20).

Jesus repeated his word of peace to them and then gave a commission to them. His peace had more meaning since his death and resurrection. In Jesus they could know real peace. And the commission was that they were to carry on his work of revelation and redemption. Just as the Father had sent him into the world to reveal God and to redeem persons, Jesus sent them into the world to make God known and to carry a redemptive message (v. 21). The mission was an extension of his mission.

Having commissioned them, Jesus also empowered them for the task he had called them to do. He breathed on them and said to them, "Receive the Holy Spirit" (v. 22). The power they would need for the mission of revelation and redemption was through the Holy Spirit. Jesus had promised them his Spirit of holiness and power (16:7-11). Now he had both equipped and empowered them for their mission in the world.

As the believers in Christ Jesus went out into the world they had a message of forgiveness of sin to proclaim (v. 23). Those persons who responded in faith to the Christ who forgave sins would have their sins forgiven. Those who refused him remained in their sin. The believers had the authority to pronounce this message of forgiveness. The construction of the words is such that the sins they forgave had already been forgiven. God had made forgiveness possible in Jesus Christ. Commissioned Christians, all Christians, have the authority to proclaim this message.

To Thomas (20:24-29).—When Jesus had appeared to the disciples on the first Easter evening one of them had been absent. Thomas was also known as the Twin. Perhaps preferring to take his grief alone, Thomas was not with the group of believers when Jesus had appeared to them (v. 24). Of course they shared that information with him when they next saw him. The good news that Jesus had risen from the dead was too good to keep. So they told Thomas that they had seen the Lord and probably also told him all that Jesus had told them (v. 25).

Not easily swayed or quickly convinced of that which seemed impossible, Thomas declared that he would not believe in the resurrection unless he could see Jesus with his own eyes and touch the wounds in his hands and side with his own hands. Their testimony that Jesus had showed them those wounds was not enough to convince him. On the next Sunday evening, one full week later, using the Jewish method of reckoning time, Thomas was with the group. Again, suddenly and without explanation, Jesus was in their midst, even though the doors were closed. He gave his greeting of peace (v. 26).

Then addressing Thomas directly Jesus instructed him to put his finger in the nailprints of the hands and his hand on the spear wound in the side (v. 27). There is no indication whether Thomas followed those instructions. Jesus did not remonstrate with Thomas about his hesitancy. He did tell Thomas not to be faithless but to be believing (v. 27).

Thomas believed. He said, "My Lord and my God!" (v. 28). While Jesus had been called "Lord" earlier, this is the only reference in John's Gospel to Jesus having been called God. To Thomas the identification was complete. Jesus was not only his Lord, he was truly God. This is the complete Christian confession. Thomas did not know how Jesus knew what he had demanded for proof. But he did know that the same Jesus he had followed, that he had seen crucified, had now stood before him and offered him the proof that he had demanded himself. He needed no more proof. Jesus was indeed both Lord over life and the God who had given life. Jesus was the incarnation of God, God who had come to earth in human flesh.

Jesus acknowledged that confession. He said that Thomas had believed on him because he had seen him. There would be many other people who would not have the opportunity to see him, to have their doubts brushed away as conclusively as Thomas' had been, who would also believe. Those people who believe on Jesus due to the witness and testimony of others (which Thomas had refused to do) would be blessed in their belief (v. 29).

If, as some believe, the epilogue of chapter 21 was written later, then the last words addressed to Jesus in the Gospel of John as originally written may have been the complete Christian confession of Thomas: "My Lord and my God."

Reason (20:30-31)

The final statement is not simply the conclusion of the last portion of the Gospel account but is both a conclusion and a climax for the whole Gospel. In these two verses the Gospel writer gave his reason for writing the Gospel.

In giving his reason for writing the Gospel, the writer shared his